GOOD NEWS

IT'S SO GOOD

THE BAD NEWS

DOESN'T MATTER

Greg Fritz

Harrison House

Tulsa, OK

Scripture quotations marked (Johnson's Paraphrase) are taken from The Heart of Paul, A Rational Paraphrase of the New Testament, Johnson, Ben Campbell. Copyright © 1976 Word Books. Used by permission. All rights reserved.

Quotations from Two Kinds of Righteousness, E. W. Kenyon, copyright ©1942 E. W. Kenyon. Used by permission of Kenyon's Gospel Publishing Society. All rights reserved.

21 20 19 18   10 9 8 7 6 5 4 3 2 1

Good News
It's So Good the Bad News Doesn't Matter
ISBN: 978-1-68031-207-2
© 2018 by Greg Fritz

Published by Harrison House Publishers
Tulsa, Oklahoma 74145
www.harrisonhouse.com

(Previously published as 978-1-53933-735-5)

CONTENTS

As cold water to a weary soul, So is good news from a far country.

—Proverbs 25:25

INTRODUCTION

Not long after the fall of the Iron Curtain in 1989, I was invited to teach in a Bible school in St. Petersburg, Russia. The late Pastor Billy Joe Daugherty from Tulsa, Oklahoma, was conducting monthly crusades and seeing thousands of Russians come to the Lord Jesus during that time. A Bible school was soon started to help educate these new believers, and I was asked to come minister morning and evening for one month. I had the privilege of teaching these new converts the story of our redemption and introducing them to the God they had just accepted. It was unlike any experience I've ever had.

For 75 years these precious people had been told there was no God. Then suddenly, they believed in God, but they knew absolutely nothing about Him. I started with the creation of the world and taught them about a God who loved them, a Savior who died for them and a place called Heaven that awaited them. They sat on the edge of their seats listening as I shared the Good News from the beginning. They wept as they learned how much God loved them and just how good the Good News really is.

GOOD NEWS

After every session, they rushed to the front to hug me, kiss me and give me little post cards and flowers to express their appreciation for the truths they were hearing. I was overwhelmed with emotion every day as I tried to put into words what is undoubtedly the greatest story ever told. I tried to imagine what it was like for them to hear these truths for the very first time, and I realized that the gospel message is so good, it almost seems too good to be true. I felt privileged to know such truths and incredibly honored to teach them to others.

I was changed during that month, and I developed a deep love for the gospel message that continues to this day. It's easy to take for granted the things we've heard and known about God for so many years, but this message is unlike any other. It's the most valuable treasure on the earth, and we've been entrusted with it. We must tell the world the Good News.

A steady stream of bad news covers every corner of the globe these days. With the introduction of the Internet and other forms of mass communication, bad news can be sent to every nook and cranny of the world minutes after it happens. But while bad news seems to sell, it's bad for us. Focusing on all the negative events that happen on a daily basis is unhealthy. It's also depressing and paralyzing.

Yet, God has Good News for us all, and it has the opposite effect. It uplifts. It liberates. And it's here to stay; it doesn't come and go from day to day. It started before creation and will last through eternity. Angels first announced this plan that's older than time itself in the New Testament.

...The angel reassured them. "Don't be afraid!" he said. "I bring you good news that will bring great joy to all people."

—Luke 2:10 (NLT)

The Good News is still for us today. If bad news has gotten you down, it's time to refocus. There's no shortage of good news; it just doesn't get as much coverage. This isn't about ignoring reality because the Good News *is* reality. It's about recognizing that many times bad news isn't accurate, doesn't last and isn't nearly as powerful as the Good News. In fact, eventually there won't be any bad news left; the Good News will swallow it up.

Actually, the Good News is so good, the bad news doesn't matter.

That's why every Christian should take time to get happy and stay happy over God's Good News. It will help you figure out where you came from, why you're here, who you are and where you're going. The answers to these questions will boost your confidence and anchor your soul in troubled times. The answer to these questions is the Good News. I invite you to read the pages that follow to find out why the Good News is so good.

~ Greg Fritz

CHAPTER 1

IN THE BEGINNING

The Bible begins with one simple opening statement, "In the beginning God created the heavens and the earth" (Genesis 1:1). What an incredible way to begin. This statement settles the argument about how the world came into existence and answers a very big question still debated today. Even more, the fact that God created the heavens and the earth is good news for us all. It wasn't an accident. The earth was created for a purpose by a Creator who had a plan. Your life has meaning because God created the heavens and the earth.

In fact, notice what the Bible goes on to say in Genesis 1.

> *Then God said, "Let there be lights in the firmament of the heavens to divide the day from the night; and let them be for signs and seasons, and for days and years; and let them be for lights in the firmament of the heavens to give light on the earth"; and it was so.*
>
> —Genesis 1:14-15

According to the Bible, the stars in the sky, the sun and the moon were created to give light on the earth. The universe is so vast we can't even see to the edges. The size of our own galaxy is almost incomprehensible at 100,000 light years across, and it contains over 100 billion stars. Astronomers believe there are billions upon billions of galaxies just like our own Milky Way in the universe.

> "Creation reveals that God is big, beautiful and precise."

These solar lights signify times and seasons. Without them, we wouldn't know what time it is. God created the whole universe for the earth. He wanted a place for the earth to exist—a sun to warm it, a moon to orbit it and a solar system to secure it in space. God wanted the earth to have a galaxy to call home and a universe to surround it.

The book of Romans tells us that the creation of the world also reveals something important about God.

> For since the creation of the world His invisible attributes are clearly seen, being understood by the things that are made, even His eternal power and Godhead....
>
> —Romans 1:20

Creation reveals that God is big, beautiful and precise. God has unlimited resources to draw upon, and this is reflected by His works. God is rich, and all of creation reveals it. Believing God's account of creation in Genesis is the key to having a proper world view. It is truly good news. Our lives have meaning because God created the heavens and the earth. Our lives have meaning because we were created; we didn't just happen.

The way you view the world and its origin is very important. I've heard people say, "We would be very selfish to think that in this vast universe, the earth is the only inhabited planet." If there is another planet out there that has life, the Bible says nothing about it. Genesis seems to imply that this is the only one. God's Word clearly says that all the stars were placed in the firmament or heavens for times and seasons and to give light on the earth.

I'm amazed at how our scientists have sought so diligently to find life somewhere else, anywhere else. It's as if it's unacceptable for the earth to be the only place in the universe where life exists. In fact, some are sure there's life on other planets; they just think we haven't found it yet. I heard one scientist interviewed, and when asked about the existence of alien life on other planets, she said, "I just can't take that possibility off the table." However, people seem eager to take the possibility that there is a God off the table. If some of these people would look for God as diligently as they look for aliens, they would make an incredible discovery that would really help the world.

This may well be the only inhabited planet in the universe. If God wanted to make a limitless universe filled with unimaginable wealth just to provide a place to hang the earth, He didn't have to ask for permission. He's God. He can do what He wants.

Rejecting the truth that God created the heavens and the earth is a big mistake. It destroys faith in God, it removes Him from our thinking and replaces Him with nothing. Therefore, life has no meaning. If life was just an accident, then we were not planned. This robs life of any purpose and robs us of our value. This kind of thinking is unacceptable to God. He has provided more than enough evidence of His existence for everyone to at least believe that He is.

Notice what the apostle Paul has to say on this topic.

> *They know the truth about God because he has made it obvious to them. For ever since the world was created, people have seen the earth and sky. Through everything God made, they can clearly see his invisible qualities—his eternal power and divine nature. So they have no excuse for not knowing God.*
>
> —Romans 1:19-20 (NLT)

This verse tells us there is enough evidence for every person to accept the fact that God is. In other words, science is no excuse for denying God's existence. People who deny the existence of God today are without excuse according to the Bible. They may be sincere in their beliefs, but it costs dearly to have a world view where God doesn't exist.

Notice the next few verses in Romans 1.

...As a result, their minds became dark and confused. Claiming to be wise, they instead became utter fools.

—Romans 1:21-22 (NLT)

It gets even worse.

Since they thought it foolish to acknowledge God, he abandoned them to their foolish thinking and let them do things that should never be done. Their lives became full of every kind of wickedness....

—Romans 1:28-29 (NLT)

If there is no God, there is no higher power to define right and wrong. There are no boundaries that can be definite and absolute. Everything can be argued and debated. The truth is subject to change. Lines clearly defined by God and the Bible are erased. There is no clear definition of morality, marriage, what defines a man or a woman or the difference between humans and animals. In fact, we have serious disagreements about these subjects today simply because people refuse to believe that "in the beginning God created the heavens and the earth."

Everyone has a right to believe what he or she wants, but just because the theory of evolution is popular in science and society does not mean it's true or factual. Ascribing to the theory of evolution is just as much an act of faith as believing in the God of creation.

I was out shopping for a house one day, and as I drove up to a home that interested me, the next door neighbor came out to greet me. He was happy to take me around his neighbor's yard and tell me everything he knew about the house. It didn't take long for him to ask me about my occupation. When I told him I was a preacher, he seemed pleased, and we went on with our tour.

Before I left, I told him I was still interested in purchasing the home as long as he didn't mind living next to a preacher. He replied that he was fine with that arrangement as long as I didn't mind living next to an atheist. I was shocked. I don't think I had ever seen an atheist and certainly never talked to one. He was very nice and didn't seem to mind that I believed in God. He explained his position by saying he was a scientist and, therefore, an atheist. Supposedly, science believes only what can be proven. I did not buy the house, so we didn't get to have any further discussion, but his position has troubled me ever since. Many scientists refuse to believe there is a God who created the heavens and the earth because they can't prove it. However, they can't prove God didn't create the heavens and the earth, and some want us to believe that.

The theory of evolution is an attempt to explain the origin of a world that obviously exists, while denying the existence of God. Unfortunately, many people want to deny the existence of God because they're unwilling to be accountable to God. They are predisposed to accept any scenario that doesn't include Him.

I heard one scientist on television trying to explain the origin of life, and it was almost embarrassing. One theory she promoted was that the original "living cell" that evolved into all life as we know it came from a mineral-rich underwater geyser deep within the earth.

The fact that science has yet to turn non-living minerals into living cells didn't seem to matter. It also didn't seem to matter that the only place on the earth where life doesn't exist is deep within the earth.

The next theory was even more incredible. The scientist suggested life could have arrived on the earth inside an asteroid from outer space. Theoretically, the asteroid was broken when it hit the ground. The living cells inside were released, and life began on the earth. I have two questions. Number one, how did the living cells inside the asteroid originate? Number two, isn't that how Superman came to the earth? It would be funny if it wasn't so pathetic.

Since no human was there in the beginning, no version of what happened can be proven, which is where evolution has let us down. It's one thing to talk about fossils and long lost species, and I appreciate true scientific discoveries. Yet, the key is the origin of life in the beginning. How did it all begin?

People who do not believe in God believe that everything that exists came from nothing. They believe that in the beginning, for no apparent reason, there was a big bang or some chemical reaction, and life began by accident. They believe everything that is, came from nothing, for no reason. I just can't take that leap of faith. This chance explosion can't be explained and can't be duplicated. In fact, the second law of thermodynamics says that order descends into disorder. This "accidental explosion" thinking goes against the laws of physics. It goes against the laws of nature, and it goes against common sense.

I don't want to argue with true science; that's not my department. I respect the work of science and appreciate the contributions science has made to the modern world. At the same time, no one can deny there was a beginning. Everyone knows that no one was there to witness what happened, so exactly what happened cannot be proven by science.

The definition of *science,* according to the Merriam-Webster Dictionary, is this: *knowledge about or study of the natural world based on facts learned through experiments and observation.* Science can study what is here, but it cannot tell us how it got here. No human was there to observe the origin of life; therefore, what happened must be believed. That's faith—not science.

I'm not trying to change science. I want to help people have faith in God. I don't want to cross the line from faith to science, but people who say with absolute certainty there is no God are crossing the line from science to faith.

How could a universe so orderly, so interconnected and perfectly suited for life happen accidentally? These people have more faith in nothing than many Christians have in God. The animal kingdom, the plant kingdom, the water cycle, the weather patterns, the orbits of the earth and moon in space, the beautiful colors of the trees, the sky and the ocean all proclaim the existence of God.

To say that the world as we know it is just an accident, and there is no God, is a step of faith I'm not willing to take. I'm familiar with accidents; I've had plenty. Rarely, if ever, do they turn out well. Rather than to believe that everything happened accidentally for no reason, it seems more logical to believe that "in the beginning God created the heavens and the earth." I've heard many origin of life scenarios, and God creating the heavens and the earth makes more sense than them all.

Even pagan tribes with no access to literature or the modern world believe in the existence of God. People who have never heard of God, never been educated or learned to read believe in God. And they should. All of creation testifies of God's existence.

> *The heavens proclaim the glory of God. The skies display his craftsmanship. Day after day they continue to speak; night after night they make him known.*
>
> —Psalms 19:1-2 (NLT)

The voice of the heavens has been communicating since the beginning of time to people from every tribe, tongue and nation the message that God exists. There is an abundance of evidence to suggest that long lost people groups have believed in a supernatural, invisible God who is responsible for the creation of the universe.

Look with me at how another Bible translation words Romans 1:20.

> *By taking a long and thoughtful look at what God has created, people have always been able to see what their eyes as such can't see: eternal power, for instance, and the mystery of his divine being. So nobody has a good excuse.*
>
> —Romans 1:20 (The MSG)

Anyone with any sense should be able to walk outside and take a look around and realize that something or someone is responsible for what they see. It has taken hundreds of years of higher education and modern "enlightenment" to rob mankind of its common sense. Genesis 1:1 confirms what everyone already knows instinctively, "In the beginning God created the heavens and the earth."

God didn't set the bar very high when it comes to finding Him. He wants to be reachable, and He has made Himself accessible to anyone and everyone. The secret to finding God is first to believe that He is. Hebrews 11:6 says, "…He who comes to God must believe that He is…."

This is the first step. No one can begin their search for God without this step. Creation plays a vital role in helping people find God by testifying of His existence. To deny that God is the Creator is to stop the search for God before it even begins. This happens in classrooms around the world every day. Yet, the Good News begins with these words: *In the beginning God created the heavens and the earth.* It only gets better from there.

CHAPTER 2

THE PURPOSE OF PLANET EARTH

The galaxy may be full of planets, but none are quite like the earth. The earth is special. God skillfully created a universe full of spectacular light shows all for the purpose of serving and supporting the earth. The earth is important to God because He created it to support life. According to Genesis, the whole universe was created by God for the earth. It was carefully designed by God to give light to the earth and to support life on the earth.

> *God set them [the stars] in the firmament of the heavens to give light on the earth.*
>
> —Genesis 1:17 (brackets mine)

The universe serves as the earth's support system. It's no coincidence that the earth is just the right distance from the sun for life to exist. It's no coincidence that the earth's climate is the only planet we know of suitable for the existence of life. Clearly, God created this planet for you and me.

Human life, animal life and plant life all find conditions necessary to sustain life on this planet. After God separated the land from the water, which He called earth and sea, He continued the creation process with plants and animals.

> *And God called the dry land Earth, and the gathering together of the waters He called Seas. And God saw that it was good. Then God said, "Let the earth bring forth grass, the herb that yields seed, and the fruit tree that yields fruit according to its kind, whose seed is in itself, on the earth"; and it was so.*

—Genesis 1:10-11

Notice the next few verses.

> *So God created great sea creatures and every living thing that moves, with which the waters abounded, according to their kind, and every winged bird according to its kind. And God saw that it was good. And God blessed them, saying, "Be fruitful and multiply, and fill the waters in the seas, and let birds multiply on the earth." ...And God made the beast of the earth according to its kind, cattle according to its kind, and everything that creeps on the earth according to its kind. And God saw that it was good.*

—Genesis 1:21-22, 25

God placed an abundance of animal and plant life on the earth that still exists to this day. What an amazing array of creatures big and small that inhabit the earth! The varieties are nearly endless. There are more than 70 million different species of animals that have been discovered with many yet to be found, and they occupy and breed in the ecosystem, just as they were designed to do from the beginning.

> "Everything God made was put into the care of mankind, and all creation was made to provide for mankind."

Then after the wonderful act of creation when all other forms of life had been created and everything was in place and ready, God created His ultimate species: man and woman.

> *So God created man in His own image; in the image of God He created him; male and female He created them. Then God blessed them, and God said to them, "Be fruitful and multiply; fill the earth and subdue it; have dominion over the fish of the sea, over the birds of the air, and over every living thing that moves on the earth."*
>
> —Genesis 1:27-28

Everything God made was put into the care of mankind, and all creation was made to provide for mankind. God gave Adam and Eve dominion over all He had made. In other words, we were made to live on the earth, and the earth was made for our use.

Consider the words of the psalmist.

> *When I consider Your heavens, the work of Your fingers, The moon and the stars, which You have ordained, What is man that You are mindful of him, And the son of man that You visit him? For You have made him a little lower than the angels, And You have crowned him with glory and honor. You have made him to have dominion over the works of Your hands; You have put all things under his feet, All sheep and oxen—Even the beasts of the field, The birds of the air, And the fish of the sea That pass through the paths of the seas. O Lord, our Lord, How excellent is Your name in all the earth!*

—Psalms 8:3-9

We aren't an imposition on planet Earth. *It was made for us.* Some people think, if it weren't for mankind, the earth would be a happy, perfect place. But the truth is, if it weren't for us, there would be no planet Earth.

More than Enough

Everything we would need through the ages was placed here, waiting to be discovered in due time. Inventions, discoveries and knowledge advancements in every field are part of God's plan for His man. It is part of the command God gave Adam and Eve when He told them to "have dominion." For that reason, it isn't wrong for mankind to use the resources God put here for our good.

God has the incredible advantage of doing everything He does with perfect foreknowledge, and He knew what we would need before we were made. He is never surprised. He was aware of the mess we would make, the carbon footprint we would leave and the pollution that would result from our being here. It was all factored into His design. It's no surprise.

In the same way, expecting parents make plans for the arrival of a new baby. They lovingly prepare a nursery by painting a room with the right colors and decorating with pictures, toys and stuffed animals. They purchase just the right crib to keep their baby safe at night. They stock up on supplies, clothes and diapers. Yet, God is a better provider than any parent who ever lived, and He spared no expense preparing for His new family. You aren't clothed and fed today because of your great skills or super intelligence. Your loving, heavenly Father put everything you would need in place long before your arrival, and He is working behind the scenes to make sure your needs are met.

Actually, you have His Word on it.

And my God shall supply all your need according to His riches in glory by Christ Jesus.

—Philippians 4:19

God has generously supplied for you. The earth is filled with abundance. This is one of God's invisible attributes seen clearly in creation. Romans 1:20 says, "For since the creation of the world His invisible attributes are clearly seen, being understood by the things that are made...." He is El Shaddai, which in Hebrew means *the God that is more than enough*. God's creation is full of abundance. It's such a relief to believe in God. When you know the Creator, you know He never comes up short. There is plenty of everything here for your consumption and mine.

It must be disturbing for people who don't believe in God, because if there is no God, then what we see is all there is. And if this is all there is, it must last forever. If that were true, then we would need to conserve and save because we would be living in a finite world. Saving the planet would become a great concern. Thank God, that's not the case.

> "God was buying dinner, and it was all you can eat."

No doubt, there are many good-intentioned people who are sincere in their desire to save the planet, and I'm definitely not saying we should trash the planet. Of course, we should be good stewards of the environment and do our part to clean up our messes. Yet, sometimes I question the motives of those who push this idea of conservation—especially when my conservation increases their bottom line.

Yet, when you know there is a God, you know what we see is not all there is. The earth will not last forever; it is temporary. It will one day be destroyed, and God will make a new one.

And: "You, Lord, in the beginning laid the foundation of the earth, And the heavens are the work of Your hands. They will perish, but

You remain; And they will all grow old like a garment; Like a cloak You will fold them up, And they will be changed. But You are the same, And Your years will not fail."

—Hebrews 1:10-12

God is the God of abundance. When that day comes and all things come to an end, there will be water left no one drank. There will be gold in the ground no one found. There will be food no one ate. There will be resources left over no one used because He is the God who is more than enough. Our view of the future changes dramatically when we believe the Good News starts with "in the beginning God created the heavens and the earth."

Multiplying Resources

The story of the loaves and fish in Matthew 14 is a great example of God's abundance. The people had been with Jesus until late in the day, and the disciples urged Jesus to send them away to buy food in the villages.

But Jesus said to them, "They do not need to go away. You give them something to eat."

—Matthew 14:16

The crowd was numbered at 5,000 men, besides women and children. Even with the modern conveniences of today, the feeding of that many people at the last minute would be almost an impossible task. The disciples thought for sure they could convince Jesus to send them away by sharing with Him how little they had, so they said to Him, "...We have here only five loaves and two fish" (Matthew 14:17).

Jesus wasn't phased and said, "...Bring them here to Me" (verse 18). The passage goes on to say,"Then He commanded the multitudes to sit down on the grass. And He took the five loaves and the two fish, and looking up to heaven, He blessed and broke and gave the loaves to the disciples; and the disciples gave to the multitudes" (Verse 19).

Look with me at a few verses further in the chapter.

So they all ate and were filled, and they took up twelve baskets full of the fragments that remained.

—Matthew 14:20

God provided an impromptu lunch for thousands of people. Notice it does not say everyone got one helping, and all the food was gone. They all ate until they *were filled.* Surely some people came back for seconds and maybe thirds before they were filled. It seemed there was no limit. God was buying dinner, and it was all you can eat. That says something about God. It says He's a God of abundance.

Then they took up 12 baskets full of leftovers. Think about it. God could have made the ratio of people to food come out even, so when the last person ate the last bite, it would have all been eaten. He could have provided just enough for each person to get a little, and He could have sent them away hungry but not starving. But that's not how God operates. The meal was provided in abundance. It was a picture of abundance, just like creation.

The meal that day was a living example of Luke 6.

> *Give, and it will be given to you: good measure, pressed down, shaken together, and running over will be put into your bosom. For with the same measure that you use, it will be measured back to you."*
>
> —Luke 6:38

The God of abundance created all things, and He put plenty of everything here for our use. We should certainly be good stewards of the planet and do our best to live responsibly, but in the end, the world is temporary and will be burned up by fire, which we'll talk about later. Until then, we have enough of everything here to take care of everyone's needs. That's good news.

CHAPTER 3

WHY MAN?

If the universe was made for the earth, and the earth was made for mankind, then why is man here? Is man part of a great cosmic accident? Is our very existence hanging by a thread? Are we just insignificant specks in the universe without purpose or meaning? The good news is that our existence was planned from the beginning. We are the objects of God's affection, and everything around us was carefully and lovingly prepared before our arrival. The entire creation is here to support human life—to support us. After each stage of creation, God said what He had made was good. Yet, after God formed man and woman, He said His creation was very good.

> *Then God saw everything that He had made,*
> *and indeed it was very good. So the evening*
> *and the morning were the sixth day.*
>
> —Genesis 1:31

Think about it. God wanted *you*. Everything else on the earth is here because you and I would need it. This makes man and woman precious. Your life isn't simply the result of millions of years of evolution, God wanted you. He planned for you. He provided for you, and He is directly responsible for your existence. You are not an accident, no matter what your parents might have told you!

> "God's dream is that every one of us—from the least to the greatest—should know Him personally."

You and I are part of a bigger plan. It's bigger than the nations. It's greater than the ambitions or desires of man. We are in the middle of God's plan. He is called the Father, and He's shown us a Father's heart from the beginning. The Father wanted a family to love, to fellowship with and to enjoy. God had a dream, and we are the fulfillment of His dream.

So often, we think and talk about our dreams and plans for the future, but we need to think about God's dream. He dreamed of having a family. God wanted children, so He began creating. We are here as the result of His dream. You can see His heart in the scriptures.

> *None of them shall teach his neighbor, and none his brother, saying, 'Know the Lord,' for all shall know Me, from the least of them to the greatest of them.*
>
> —Hebrews 8:11

God doesn't want to be a far-off, unknown God. He wants a personal relationship with people. God loves people. He doesn't want anyone to just hear about Him or be taught about Him by another. God's dream is that every one of us—from the least to the greatest—should know Him personally.

In fact, 2 Corinthians 6 tells us that God desires more than for us to just know Him.

> *Therefore "Come out from among them and be separate, says the Lord. Do not touch what is unclean, and I will receive you. I will be a Father to you, and you shall be My sons and daughters, says the Lord Almighty."*
>
> —2 Corinthians 6:17-18

These verses were Old Testament verses that were quoted again in the New Testament to reveal the love of the Father from the beginning. His greatest desire for people is that we know Him as a Father. This is God's dream that's existed since before time began. He wants a family, and that's why we're all here. Friend, that's good news! The truth is, no Father has ever loved His children more than God does.

> *Behold what manner of love the Father has bestowed on us, that we should be called children of God!*
>
> —1 John 3:1

God loves us more than we can even imagine. He doesn't want us to simply exist as His servants; God wants us to be His children. He could have related to us any way He wanted. We could have been associates, partners or employees of God. He could have related to us as a great uncle or a divine acquaintance with little or no commitment to our needs or our wellbeing, but those relationships weren't good enough for the Father God. There is only one relationship where the recipient gets more than he'll ever give in return. It is a relationship that is often a one-way street: the parent-child relationship. That is the only arrangement that would satisfy the heart of God.

Children get the best of what a parent can give. Parents spend the best years of their lives raising their children, and they provide them with the best they have to offer. Parents eagerly go through the stress of childbirth and the babyhood stage of development with the crying, the diapers and the nighttime feedings. Then come the teenage years that often can be awkward. There have even been accounts where teenage kids who were provided clothes, food, a free place to live, cell phones, cars and even a free education, were embarrassed to be seen with their own parents in public! Parents the world over make huge sacrifices to raise their children. They do it gladly, without the promise of being thanked or, at times, even appreciated.

God knew that those days would come in His experience with His family, but it didn't stop Him from pursuing His dream. Nothing less was acceptable to our Father who the scripture says, "...chose us in Him from the foundation of the world..." (Ephesians 1:4).

The sacrifices a parent makes can't be put into numbers or valued in dollars, and no parent would even expect to be repaid for the work of parenting. If your children asked to repay you, you'd be insulted because it was never about the money and never will be. Parenting is not a business arrangement. If children were employees, they probably would have been fired. If they were partners, the partnership would have been dissolved. If they were associates, by now, they would have been unassociated. But they are children, so they get it all for nothing. Parents would not have it any other way.

Likewise, God is the ultimate Father and has chosen to invest His time, effort and resources in us. We can never repay Him for giving us the gift of life and the opportunity to know Him as our Father. He doesn't expect repayment. What He wants out of it is us—our love, our attention, our worship.

The story of the prodigal son perfectly illustrates God's true motive for creating you and me. The younger son in the story reached an age where he wanted to experience life on his own without his father's input. He wanted to do his own thing without answering to anyone. He didn't want his father involved in his life, so he took his inheritance and went out into the world.

The next few verses in Luke tell us the son ran into a few problems.

> *And not many days after, the younger son gathered all together, journeyed to a far country, and there wasted his possessions with prodigal living. But when he had spent all, there arose a severe famine in that land, and he began to be in want.*
>
> —Luke 15:13-14

25

He had wasted all that he had in no time and ended up working on a pig farm. The son soon realized that his father's servants had it better than he did, so he returned home ashamed and humiliated. He had a pitiful speech prepared to give his father on his return.

> *And he arose and came to his father. But when he was still a great way off, his father saw him and had compassion, and ran and fell on his neck and kissed him. And the son said to him, 'Father, I have sinned against heaven and in your sight, and am no longer worthy to be called your son.'*
>
> —Luke 15:20-21

The young son on his way home was prepared to serve his father as a hired hand or servant. He realized he had wasted his inheritance and made a mockery of the family name. He had not gotten an education. He had not trained for new skills. He wasted his opportunity to become something. Worse yet, the son was sure his father would reject him because of it, but he misjudged the father's love. The father would have shared his son's joy of becoming a businessman or a scholar. He would have been proud for his son to make his mark in the world. But first and foremost, the father wanted a son. Above all else, the father wanted a son.

So did the father tell his servants to reject the home-bound son? No. The father prepared a homecoming in grand style:

> *"But the father said to his servants, 'Bring out the best robe and put it on him, and put a*

*ring on his hand and sandals on his feet. And
bring the fatted calf here and kill it, and let
us eat and be merry; for this my son was dead
and is alive again; he was lost and is found.'
And they began to be merry.*

—Luke 15:22-24

The son misunderstood the relationship and put pressure on himself to perform or to try to earn the father's love, not realizing he already had it. He had the father's love, not because of what he did, but because of who he was. The father was not nearly as interested in the son's failures or successes as he was in having him home again. The father was thrilled because he got his son back.

There was a turning point in my life when I realized I may not have been the greatest or the smartest or the most successful person who ever lived, but I knew I could be a son. And that's what the heavenly Father wanted me to be above all else.

Your relationship with your earthly father may have been a very bad experience. Maybe you don't even know who your biological father is. Maybe you were abused by your father. Maybe you were neglected when you needed your father the most. These experiences are all too common in this fallen world, and they drive people away from God. For people who have encountered such circumstances, even the thought of a heavenly Father causes fear and anger because their only example of a father was such a failure.

But, friend, please don't let what a man on the earth has done rob you of the love of your Father in heaven. Earthly fathers are given the privilege and the responsibility to represent the Father God in the lives of their children for a short time. They serve temporarily as earthly substitutes for the heavenly Father. Their primary job is to share with their children the love of a father and teach them how to relate to a father until they are old enough to have a personal relationship with God, the true Father.

Since the fall of man, every human father has fallen short of the mark at some time or another. None have proven to be the perfect father, and some have failed in this monumental task more than others. I'm sure every earthly father would agree that we've all failed in one way or another in fulfilling the fatherhood role in the lives of our children. Many fathers are too young to grasp the importance of their role, and most have never been taught by precept or example.

Whether your earthly father was a good father, a bad father or no father at all, you have a right to experience the love of God as the true and eternal Father. This is God's will for you and every other person on earth. Don't let past experiences rob you of the love of your heavenly Father. He has never let you down or done anything to hurt you. His will for you is only good. Let Him define the love of a father in your life. We were created to be the children of God, and there is nothing in life that fulfills you like being what you were made to be.

God wants us to experience the best He has to offer. Not even the angels have a relationship with God like we humans have. Our special place in God is reserved only for human beings. Those who have been born again and accepted God's offer of redemption through Jesus Christ become the children of God.

We find another scripture that reveals God's dream for mankind in Ephesians 1:

> *Just as He chose us in Him before the foundation of the world, that we should be holy and without blame before Him in love, having predestined us to adoption as sons by Jesus Christ to Himself, according to the good pleasure of His will.*
>
> —Ephesians 1:4-5

Think about it. God chose us before the foundation of the world. He had this dream for a long time, which is just one more proof that the universe is not an accident. It was planned long before it ever began, and everything God made, He made with us in mind.

If the universe is here for the earth, and the earth is here for man, then why is man here?

There's just one reason: God's love for us.

Everything that you can see is here because of the love of God. The force behind all of creation is love. We are part of a love project. John 3:16 says, "For God *so loved* the world...." And He still does. He hasn't changed His mind. God is in love with people, and love is the reason for all of creation.

The next time you look at the stars above or the blue sky or the trees or the mountains or the ocean or a beautiful lawn, filled with green grass and flowers, remember it is all here because of God's love for *you*. We tend to forget the bigger picture as life rushes on, and we face the challenges life presents. The Good News is that the force behind everything that is, is love. Nothing will ever change that.

CHAPTER 4

THE ENTRANCE OF EVIL

We've read from Genesis 1 how God created a literal paradise in the garden of Eden and then crowned his stunning achievement with Adam and Eve, who were also perfect and created to live eternally. God Himself would come to walk and fellowship with them, face to face. There was no death there, nothing to hurt or abuse or kill. Life for them was heaven on Earth.

So what happened? If there is a God, why is there so much evil in the world?

That question has been asked over and over, by many through the ages. In fact, it's one of the questions asked by the atheist and the agnostic to excuse their position of denying the existence of God, despite the testimony of creation itself.

Let's look at God's Word to find the answer. The Word of God has all the answers. Begin with me in Psalm 8 to see God's plan for man from the beginning.

What is man that You are mindful of him, and the son of man that You visit him? For

You have made him a little lower than the angels, and You have crowned him with glory and honor.

—Psalm 8:4-5

That word *angels* in the Hebrew is *elohim* which is the Hebrew word for *God*. Mankind was made just a shade lower than God. Man was made a spirit like his Father God who is called the father of spirits (Hebrews 12:9). This man was not some half-developed Neanderthal man. After God created Adam, He had Adam name all the animals, over 70 million species that we know of today. It would take a brilliant mind to do that. Man was created to be the friend of God, to walk with God and to fellowship with God.

As we read earlier, God immediately gave Adam and Eve dominion over all the earth and everything God had created in the world.

Then God blessed them, and God said to them, "Be fruitful and multiply; fill the earth and subdue it; have dominion over the fish of the sea, over the birds of the air, and over every living thing that moves on the earth."

—Genesis 1:28

They were permitted to eat all the herbs and fruits the garden produced, except for the Tree of the Knowledge of Good and Evil. They were given a free will, which allowed them to choose to love and to serve God or not.

And the Lord God commanded the man,
saying, "Of every tree of the garden you may
freely eat; but of the tree of the knowledge of
good and evil you shall not eat, for in the day
that you eat of it you shall surely die."

—Genesis 2:16-17

The Tree of the Knowledge of Good and Evil represented an alternative—a choice other than serving God. What good would it be for man to have a free will with the ability to choose, but only have one god or one option available? God has always wanted His children to choose Him and to love Him freely, the way He loves us. The tree represented that other choice. Yet, choosing to eat the forbidden fruit was a leap into sin. It was expressly forbidden, and it was the biggest mistake in history.

The fall of man was the result of believing lies, lies that are still being told. These lies are working to destroy people today, just as they did in the beginning. God's directions were clear. But when Satan approached Eve, he misquoted and exaggerated God's command:

He said to the woman, "Did God actually say,
'You shall not eat of any tree in the garden'?"

—Genesis 3:1 (ESV)

That's not what God said at all. God said they couldn't eat from one tree. This is a dangerous misinterpretation. It's important to read the fine print, and be sure you know what God has said. This lie insinuates that if you serve God, you cannot do anything. Your life will be boring and limited because God doesn't want you to have any fun. That's just not true. Worse yet, people still believe this lie today as it's still told in various forms.

I've had people tell me they don't want to serve God because they want to have fun. Yet, serving God is fun. It's the most rewarding, fulfilling life anyone can live. Sure there are things God doesn't want us to do. He doesn't want us to do drugs and experience addiction. He doesn't want us to live recklessly and die an early death.

There were people who tried to get me to "enjoy" life as a young person. They thought they were having all the fun and would be the first ones to say, "You can't do anything fun if you serve God." I didn't go with them to the parties and get involved in the sin and carousing, and now, looking back, I see what I missed. I didn't have a baby out of wedlock. I didn't spend any time in rehab for addiction recovery. I didn't go to jail or die young. I really missed a lot by serving God and living life His way.

The things God doesn't want us to do are bad for us. He wants the best for us, and living life His way is the best way. However, the lie that says you can't do anything if you live for God is still being told and still being believed. The enemy just recycles what works and uses it over and over.

Eve attempted to correct the serpent's understanding of God's command, as if he didn't know.

> *And the woman said to the serpent, "We may eat the fruit of the trees of the garden; but of the fruit of the tree which is in the midst of*

the garden, God has said, 'You shall not eat it, nor shall you touch it, lest you die.'"

—Genesis 3:2-3

The next lie Satan told doesn't just misinterpret what God said; it flat out contradicts what God said. Notice what the serpent said next:

...You will not surely die.

—Genesis 3:4

That was a brazen lie. God said, "in the day you eat you will surely die" (Genesis 2:17). Satan said, "You will not surely die." Who told the truth?

We've all heard this lie before. It's spoken and believed today by many people. Enticing people to sin, so-called friends often say things like, "Come on! It's not going to hurt you." "Nobody will ever know." "It doesn't matter what you do. God will love you."

It's true that God will love us, but what we do does still matter. The truth is, sin kills. God's not out to get us, but sin might. It may appear as harmless as the forbidden fruit, but there is a reason sin is wrong. God has declared it off limits because it's not best for us. Adam and Eve doubted God's Word, and every one of us has felt the effects. We're all still reeling from its effects.

The third and final lie the serpent told that day in the garden is even worse. This lie questions God's motives for giving His commands and setting boundaries for them as if He wanted to limit them or deprive them of a happy life.

Look with me at the third lie.

> *For God knows that in the day you eat of it your eyes will be opened, and you will be like God, knowing good and evil."*
>
> —Genesis 3:5

Notice what Matthew Henry had to say about this insidious statement in *Matthew Henry's Commentary on the Whole Bible:*

> *This was a great affront to God, and the highest indignity that could be done him, a reproach to his power, as if he feared his creatures, and much more a reproach to his goodness, as if he hated the work of his own hands and would not have those whom he has made to be made happy.*

"With one bite, sin entered the earth, and with sin, came evil, pain, death and suffering that continues to this day."

Satan is undermining Eve's faith in God's goodness and sowing doubt in her mind about His care for her. God was not trying to limit them in life or keep them from being like Him. He was trying to keep them from experiencing all the evils sin would bring.

Those who believe this lie today feel they must go out on their own like the prodigal son to be happy and "find themselves" as if God wants much less for them than they want for themselves or as if He's holding them back from experiencing life to the fullest. The truth is, God wants the absolute best for His children, and living life within the boundaries of His will is the only way to have it. It's the only way to really live.

Once Satan had sown doubt in Eve's mind about the motive behind God's command, the decision was made, and the first sin was committed. Adam and Eve chose to eat the forbidden fruit. They chose to sin. It was their decision and theirs alone. It was not God's fault. God told Adam not to sin and clearly explained the results of disobedience. Yet, with one bite, sin entered the earth, and with sin, came evil, pain, death and suffering that continues to this day.

God never wanted any human to die or suffer. It was not His design that humankind go through wars and natural disasters. None of this existed until man sinned. The reality of little children suffering hunger, disease and abuse was never supposed to happen in this world.

These evils, along with death and hell and the grave, are the result of sin—and mankind is solely responsible.

It's not fair for people today to look at the world and blame God for everything bad that happens. God tried to warn Adam and Eve. He was very clear about the consequences.

Adam and Eve didn't just fall into sin. They leaped in with both feet, and the world has felt the effects from that moment. Sin unleashed horrific consequences on the human race that continues to this day. God knew the full extent of what Adam had done. He also knew that in the millennia to come, man would blame God and even deny His existence. But in His great love for us, God still chose to redeem mankind and offer the gift of salvation to the human race.

The Consequences of Sin

There is a simple answer to the age-old question, *If there is a God, then why is there so much evil in the world?* The answer is this: It's man's fault.

In fact, let's look at some of the consequences of Adam's sin, and subsequently our sin, to see what it has done to the world we live in.

1. Sin brought a curse on the whole world.

> *Then to Adam He said, "Because you have heeded the voice of your wife, and have eaten from the tree of which I commanded you, saying, 'You shall not eat of it': "Cursed is the ground for your sake; In toil you shall eat of it all the days of your life."*
>
> —Genesis 3:17

On that day, life on the earth became difficult. Sweat was added to work, and the curse began to affect every area of life.

2. Sin gave Satan dominion over all of mankind.

We know that we are of God, and the whole world lies under the sway of the wicked one.

—1 John 5:19

But even if our gospel is veiled, it is veiled to those who are perishing, whose minds the god of this age has blinded, who do not believe, lest the light of the gospel of the glory of Christ, who is the image of God, should shine on them.

—2 Corinthians 4:3-4

When did Satan become the god of this age? When Adam sinned. It was Satan who tempted Eve in the garden to eat the forbidden fruit. He deceived Eve with his lies by contradicting the word of God, but he didn't deceive Adam.

For Adam was formed first, then Eve. And Adam was not deceived, but the woman being deceived, fell into transgression.

—1 Timothy 2:13-14

Adam knew what he was doing, and by sinning, he allowed Satan to set up his unholy kingdom on the earth. Because of Adam's sin, Satan has a right to be here. Jesus never told the devil or demons to leave the earth or go to the lake of fire. That will happen in the end, but now in this present age, Satan has a certain amount of time to rule. In other words, Satan has a lease on planet Earth.

Whatever amount of time God gave Adam and the human race to be fruitful, multiply, replenish the earth and take dominion over creation, was handed over to Satan in the garden. He legally became the god of this world.

You can see some of Satan's influence over the world when he confronted Jesus at the end of the 40-day fast in the wilderness.

> *Then the devil, taking Him up on a high mountain, showed Him all the kingdoms of the world in a moment of time. And the devil said to Him, "All this authority I will give You, and their glory; for this has been delivered to me, and I give it to whomever I wish. Therefore, if You will worship before me, all will be Yours."*
>
> — Luke 4:5-7

This was a legitimate temptation. If it wasn't legitimate, Jesus would have known it. This encounter with Jesus shows that Satan does have authority in this world and can share it with whomever he chooses. Unlike Adam, Jesus quoted God's Word and resisted the temptations in the wilderness.

It's really no secret that there's a devil who operates an evil kingdom in the world right now. It's the source of evil and suffering that confronts us at every turn. It's not fair, and it's not right to blame God for everything that happens in this world. It was never a part of God's plan for the earth to experience these evils. And yet, God is routinely blamed for them.

Actually, it's easy to tell who's doing what in the earth. If it kills, steals and destroys, it's the work of Satan. If it helps, blesses and gives life, it's God.

> *The thief does not come except to steal, and to kill, and to destroy. I have come that they may have life, and that they may have it more abundantly.*
>
> — John 10:10

God never intended for man to endure tornadoes, hurricanes, earthquakes and fires. Poverty, famine and disease were never God's plan for humankind. These things would have never happened on the earth if Adam hadn't sinned. The curse that sin produced has impacted the earth on every level. You can bet that Satan and his army of demons and devils are behind every unjust war and genocide. Satan glories in human suffering. But his time—just like a lease—is limited and running out.

Jesus encountered demons in land of the Gadarenes, in Matthew 8, who knew there was a time limit on their work on Earth.

> *When He had come to the other side, to the country of the Gergesenes, there met Him two demon-possessed men, coming out of the tombs, exceedingly fierce, so that no one could pass that way. And suddenly they cried out, saying, "What have we to do with You, Jesus, You Son of God? Have You come here to torment us before the time?"*
>
> —Matthew 8:28-29

41

Jesus cast those demons into a herd of swine and they troubled that man no more, and the time is coming when evil will trouble mankind no more. Satan and his army will be cast into the lake of fire forever. However, until then, the devil is still the god of this world.

3. Sin brought mankind under the influence of sin, sickness and death.

Sickness and death are not from God and were never meant to be a part of the human experience.

Romans 6:17 says, "...though you were slaves of sin..." Instead of being children of God, the human race became slaves of sin. When man fell, he fell into sin. Sin became his master, and it opened the door to sickness, disease and death.

The curse of the broken law came upon the world's inhabitants. Everyone was guilty of breaking the laws of God. All have sinned and come short of His glory, so all were under the curse of the law. This curse is clearly spelled out in Deuteronomy 28. A large portion of the curse of the law described in Deuteronomy 28 contains sickness and disease. After an exhaustive list of ailments, it says in verse 61 that it includes "every sickness and every plague, which is not written in this Book of the Law...."

4. Sin changed the very nature of man.

This is the saddest and the most devastating result

of Adam's sin in the garden. Man was no longer able to walk with God. His nature was changed. Ephesians 2:3 says, we "were by nature children of wrath, just as the others." Adam's spirit, which had been alive to God, died.

He was not the same as he was when God created him and breathed into his spirit the breath of life. He was born again in reverse. In a sense, his spirit died. The Bible calls this condition *spiritual death*, which is the absence of the life of God.

This is what God was warning Adam about in Genesis 3:17 when He said, "...but of the tree of the knowledge of good and evil you shall not eat, for in the day that you eat of it you shall surely die." In Hebrew, the phrase *you shall surely die* is more accurately translated *in dying you shall die*. This gives us the idea of a dual death. We know that Adam didn't die physically for hundreds of years, but he did die spiritually on the day he ate of the forbidden fruit. Spiritual death came before physical death.

Death in this context does not mean to cease to exist, but to have a spiritual nature void of the life of God. It is the nature of sin. Notice Ephesians 2.

> *And you He made alive, who were dead in trespasses and sins.*
>
> —Ephesians 2:1

He literally became spiritually incompatible with God. He became an enemy of God by his very nature.

In Romans 5, Paul tells us how this affected everyone:

> *Therefore, just as through one man sin entered the world, and death through sin, and thus death spread to all men, because all sinned.*
>
> —Romans 5:12

This sin nature was passed on to everyone. Adam was God's pattern or master copy, and when he became sinful, that condition was passed along to all his offspring. *Adam* means *mankind.* When Adam sinned, it was the fall of all mankind. That's why it says in Romans 3:23, "for all have sinned and fall short of the glory of God."

We can see, the immediate impact of sin on Adam and Eve was shame and fear. Never before had they felt these feelings, but sin changed them. Fear and shame were now a part of life.

> *So he said, "I heard Your voice in the garden, and I was afraid because I was naked; and I hid myself."*
>
> —Genesis 3:10

Man was not just guilty of sin, but he became a sinner. No longer could he enjoy walking and talking with God in the garden. It looked as if God's dream of having a family was dead. God could no longer allow Adam and Eve to enjoy the paradise He made for them. He forced them out of the garden, and they lived in a new world where Satan was god, and sin and death ruled. Everything had changed.

A description of fallen humanity is given in Romans 3.

> *As it is written: "There is none righteous, no, not one; There is none who understands; There is none who seeks after God. They have all turned aside; They have together become unprofitable; There is none who does good, no, not one. Their throat is an open tomb; With their tongues they have practiced deceit; The poison of asps is under their lips; Whose mouth is full of cursing and bitterness. Their feet are swift to shed blood; Destruction and misery are in their ways; And the way of peace they have not known. There is no fear of God before their eyes."*
>
> —Romans 3:10-18

It looked as if sin had forever ruined God's man and all of creation. Man's condition was incompatible with a holy God. The days of fellowship in the garden had come to an end and drastic changes were in store for Adam and Eve.

> *Therefore the Lord God sent him out of the garden of Eden to till the ground from which he was taken. So He drove out the man; and He placed cherubim at the east of the garden of Eden, and a flaming sword which turned every way, to guard the way to the tree of life.*
>
> —Genesis 3:23-24

Sin had entered the world and into the heart of man. The process of sin and death had begun. The door was opened to sickness and disease. Hatred was one of the symptoms of the sinful heart and quickly manifested in the first family when Cain killed Abel. Murder and abuse became part of the human experience as sin took root in the hearts of men.

The first day Adam sinned was the saddest day on the earth. Everything that God had made was polluted, corrupted and ruined by sin. It could have been the end of the world. God could have given up on His plan, let His dream die and destroyed the world. But that's not the kind of God we serve. He never gives up. He follows through with His plans, and even in the midst of such a tragedy, there was good news.

God announced the answer on that very day as He spoke to the serpent.

> *And I will put enmity between you and the woman, and between your seed and her Seed; He shall bruise your head, And you shall bruise His heel.*
>
> —Genesis 3:15

What this meant to the devil, was that the seed of a woman—the Savior—was coming. The answer was on the way. Before the world ever knew there was a problem, God had an answer, and His name is Jesus. This was the first announcement of God's Good News to the world. It may have looked as if Satan had won, but God was not finished yet. This story is far from over. The Good News is so good.

CHAPTER 5

OUR SUBSTITUTE

The evil and horrific consequences that came into the earth along with man's decision to sin changed almost everything. The one thing it did not change was God's great love and desire for a family. God immediately set in motion a plan—a redemption—to restore mankind. God set about a divine intervention.

It was not possible for God to ignore the sin nature that was now resident in every person born of Adam. God could not overlook sin. He is a holy God, and sin is not compatible with His nature. God wanted His family, but He could not and would not obtain it unjustly or illegally. Everything about God's plan to rescue mankind had to be done according to the rules of justice. Sin had to be dealt with legally.

Without divine intervention, man would experience the full consequences of sin that included death and hell because justice had to be satisfied. At the same time, God did not want to destroy mankind. His mercy and love found a way to save man from eternal separation from God. God's plan was to redeem us through the death of His son. The definition of *redemption* is *freedom or deliverance through the payment of a price.*

Jesus chose to pay the price for our freedom.

"The only way God could accomplish His will and satisfy the claims of justice against sin without sending the world to hell was the cross of Christ."

·The plan of redemption had to be just the right balance of mercy and judgment. God's answer was the cross of Christ. One man would pay for the sins of many. Through the cross God demonstrated "… His righteousness, that He might be *just* and the *justifier* of the one who has faith in Jesus" (Romans 3:26).

Vines Expository Dictionary of New Testament Words makes this comment about God demonstrating His righteousness:

> *"His righteousness as exhibited in the death of Christ, is sufficient to show men that God is neither indifferent to sin or regards it lightly, on the contrary, it demonstrates that quality of holiness in Him which must find expression in His condemnation of sin."*

His holiness required that He be just, and His love and mercy demanded that He be the justifier. Had God been just without being merciful, we would all have had to die for our own sins. He could have destroyed the world and washed His hands of it, but His mercy would not allow it.

> *Through the Lord's mercies we are not consumed, Because His compassions fail not.*
>
> —Lamentations 3:22

The only way God could accomplish His will and satisfy the claims of justice against sin without sending the world to hell was the cross of Christ. This was God's answer. It was the perfect combination of mercy and righteousness. The Bible speaks of the work of the cross long before it happened in Psalms.

> *Mercy and truth have met together; Righteousness and peace have kissed.*
>
> —Psalm 85:10

What a beautiful picture of redemption! It was on the cross that mercy and judgment found full expression concerning the condition of man. It was through the work of the cross that God was able to restore His man back into fellowship and undo what sin had done. The cross and the mystery of the gospel were kept secret from the foundation of the world (Romans 16:25).

"...In due time Christ died for the ungodly" (Romans 5:6). Thank God, Jesus was willing to die for us and pay the price to set us free. What Jesus did, He did for everyone. Redemption is real, and it was costly. Hebrews 12:2 says, "...who for the joy that was set before Him endured the cross, despising the shame, and has sat down at the right hand of the throne of God."

Substitution

It may seem unfair that the sin of Adam was credited to the whole human race. It may seem unfair that God created man knowing that he would sin. However, if God assumes the liabilities of the fall, He will have answered any criticism of man against Him.

Again, keep in mind that the very name *Adam* means *mankind*. Adam was the first representative man, and when he sinned, it was as if all man had sinned in him.

> *Therefore, just as through one man sin entered the world, and death through sin, and thus death spread to all men, because all sinned.*
>
> —Romans 5:12

Sin—and the sin nature—is universal. No one who descended from Adam is exempt. All have sinned and come short of the glory of God. In this sense, every human being is in the same boat. "There is none righteous, no, not one" (Romans 3:10). We were all born in sin.

Jesus is called the last Adam, and He too is a representative of all mankind. We will see how God used this same principle of substitution to set us free.

> *And so it is written, "The first man Adam became a living being." The last Adam*

became a life-giving spirit.

—1 Corinthians 15:45

The same law that allowed one man's sin to be credited to all others allows one man to pay the penalty for all men. Jesus became our substitute. The word *substitute* simply means *one who takes the place of another.*

Throughout the Epistles, we read several scriptures that reveal Jesus as our substitute. They use the word *for* because Jesus gave Himself *for us.* He stood *for us* or *in our place.* Let's look at a few substitution scriptures from Paul's epistles:

> *For He made Him who knew no sin to be sin for us, that we might become the righteousness of God in Him.*
>
> —2 Corinthians 5:21

> *For when we were still without strength, in due time Christ died for the ungodly.*
>
> —Romans 5:6

> *who gave Himself for us, that He might redeem us from every lawless deed and purify for Himself His own special people, zealous for good works.*
>
> —Titus 2:14

Who gave Himself a ransom for all, to be testified in due time.

—1 Timothy 2:6

Christ has redeemed us from the curse of the law, having become a curse for us (for it is written, "Cursed is everyone who hangs on a tree").

—Galatians 3:13

For you know the grace of our Lord Jesus Christ, that though He was rich, yet for your sakes He became poor, that you through His poverty might become rich.

—2 Corinthians 8:9

Jesus Suffered for Us

When Jesus took our place and died for us, He suffered the judgment that belonged to us. He did not die just to show us how much He loved us. He took our place and received the punishment we deserved. His death was not the death of a martyr, but that of a substitute. He paid the penalty we owed because of sin.

This is why the truth of the virgin birth is so important. Jesus was born of a virgin, so He was not born in sin because He was not a descendent of Adam. His father was God, and therefore, He was sinless. It was the value of a sinless life and His holy, spotless blood that was necessary to pay for the sins of the world. A sinner could not die for sinners. Our Savior had to be a holy, righteous sacrifice. Only Jesus qualified. He was fully man and fully God all at the same time. He was human yet righteous.

No one can really understand the pain and horror He endured as our substitute, but there are many scriptures that give us glimpses of His suffering.

Jesus knew something of the price He would pay. Notice the agony He suffered as He entered the garden of Gethsemane the night before His crucifixion.

> *...He began to be troubled and deeply distressed. Then He said to them, "My soul is exceedingly sorrowful, even to death...."*
>
> —Mark 14:33-34

Let's look at a few other translations of the same verses in Mark 14.

> *Horror and dismay came over Him.*
>
> —NEB

> *Then He took with Him Peter and James and John, and began to be full of terror and distress, and He said to them, "My heart is oppressed with anguish to the very point of death...."*
>
> —WNT

I feel grief in the depths of my being as I face death.

—Johnson's Paraphrase

He started to feel terror and grief. I am so full of sorrow, He told them, I am dying.

—Beck

The increasing realization of what lay ahead came to Him with such a sense of overwhelming shock, that He was distraught in His mind. He said, My soul is grief-stricken with a grief like unto death.

—Barclay

It was in the garden that Jesus submitted to the will of God and made His final decision to go to the cross for us. It is fitting that the last Adam made his decision to save mankind in a garden just as the first Adam made his decision to plunge humanity into to sin in a garden.

After Jesus had settled the issue, He was arrested and taken to trial. He was falsely accused and condemned by an unruly crowd. He was beaten with a Roman scourge and then endured a horrific death on the cross.

Isaiah 53:5 was written more than 700 years before Jesus was crucified, and it gives us an insight to the substitutionary work of Christ. It speaks of how His suffering paid the price, so we might have forgiveness of our sins, peace in our minds and healing for our bodies.

But He was wounded for our transgressions,
He was bruised for our iniquities; The
chastisement for our peace was upon Him,
And by His stripes we are healed.

—Isaiah 53:5

Notice that physical healing was paid for at the same time as forgiveness of sins. Healing is part of our redemption as is revealed in 1 Peter.

Who Himself bore our sins in His own body
on the tree, that we, having died to sins,
might live for righteousness—by whose
stripes you were healed.

—1 Peter 2:24

Jesus took no short cuts in His substitutionary work for us. His plan was to get back everything that sin had taken from us. He endured unimaginable pain as He submitted to the Roman scourge to pay for our healing.

The following are excerpts from Cunningham Geikie's *The Life and Words of Christ* (Public Domain):

Victims condemned to the cross first
underwent the hideous torture of the scourge,
and this was immediately inflicted on Jesus.
He was now seized by some of the soldiers
standing near, and after being stripped to the
waist, was bound in a stooping posture, His
hands being behind His back, to a post, or a
block, near the tribunal. He was then beaten
at the pleasure of the soldiers, with knots of
rope, or plaited leathern thongs, armed at

55

the ends with acorn shaped drops of lead, or small sharp pointed bones. In many cases not only was the back of the person scourged cut open in all directions, but even the eyes, the face, and the breast were torn, and teeth not seldom knocked out. Under the fury of the countless stripes, the victims sometimes sank -amidst screams, convulsive leaps, and distortions- into a senseless heap; sometimes died on the spot; sometimes were taken away, an unrecognizable mass of bleeding flesh, to find deliverance in death, from the inflammation and fever, sickness and shame.

The scourging of Jesus was of the severest, for the soldiers only too gladly vented on any Jew the grudge they bore that nation, and they would, doubtless, try if they if they could not force out the confession denied to the governor. Besides, He was to be crucified, and the harder the scourging, the less life there would be left to detain them afterwards on guard at the cross.

Eusebius an early church historian describes the scourging of some martyrs thus: "All around were horrified to see them so torn with the scourges that their very veins were laid bare, and the inner muscles and sinews, and even their very bowels were exposed."

It's hard to read these words, but it's the truth nonetheless. The payment for sin was real, and though redemption today is free, it wasn't cheap. Jesus did for us what we couldn't do for ourselves, and He paid the ultimate price that we would never have been able to pay. We get a glimpse of the high cost of sin when we see the indescribable suffering He endured.

Jesus was beaten and bloodied and then nailed to a cross. He was reviled by strangers and enemies as He was left to die.

> *Then two robbers were crucified with Him, one on the right and another on the left. And those who passed by blasphemed Him, wagging their heads and saying, "You who destroy the temple and build it in three days, save Yourself! If You are the Son of God, come down from the cross." Likewise the chief priests also, mocking with the scribes and elders, said, "He saved others; Himself He cannot save. If He is the King of Israel, let Him now come down from the cross, and we will believe Him. He trusted in God; let Him deliver Him now if He will have Him; for He said, 'I am the Son of God.'" Even the robbers who were crucified with Him reviled Him with the same thing.*
>
> —Matthew 27:38-44

The words He uttered next are some of the saddest recorded in scripture. He quoted Psalm 22:1 that was obviously written for that day and that moment. "My God, My God, why have you forsaken me?"

Then Jesus died. He did not faint or go unconscious as some have speculated. He died. This is a very important point. If He was to take our place and pay our debt, He had to die.

Make no mistake. His life was not taken. His death was voluntary. Jesus gave His life for everyone of us. By His own admission, He went to the cross to die, and that's what happened as He gave up His spirit.

In the apostle John's account of the death of Christ, we see additional evidence not included in the other Gospels that Jesus died on the cross.

> *So when Jesus had received the sour wine, He said, "It is finished!" And bowing His head, He gave up His spirit.*
>
> —John 19:30

John goes on to explain that Jewish law dictated that the bodies of executed criminals be removed from sight before sunset (Deuteronomy 21:23). So to hasten death, Roman soldiers would break the legs of the crucified. Without the use of their legs, breathing was nearly impossible, and the result was death by suffocation. The legs of the other two victims crucified that day were broken. John tells us what happened next.

> *But when they came to Jesus and saw that He was already dead, they did not break His legs.*
>
> —John 19:33

The Romans were experts at execution and death. If they had even the slightest doubt that Jesus was alive, they would have broken His legs along with the other two. Furthermore, what happened next is even more proof that Jesus died on the cross.

But one of the soldiers pierced His side with a spear, and immediately blood and water came out.

—John 19:34

This meant that the circulation of Jesus' blood had ceased long enough for the white blood cells to separate from the red blood cells as it coagulated in His lifeless body. This could only happen in a dead body with no pulse.

Jesus had died. God's plan was fulfilled. Nothing less would pay the penalty for sin, and Romans 6 tells us why.

For the wages of sin is death, but the gift of God is eternal life in Christ Jesus our Lord.

—Romans 6:23

If Jesus had not died, He would not have paid for our sins for "the wages of sin is death." We sinned. He died. That was the arrangement, and that's what happened.

The future looked very dark and hopeless at that point.

When we read in the Gospels of the disciples' confusion as they watched their Messiah die and be buried in a rich man's tomb, it's easy to understand their despair. It was as if all their dreams died on that cross. All the promises they had heard and the plans they had made with Jesus seemed to die that day. As they contemplated their future with fear and uncertainty, we come to the best part of the plan of redemption. Three days later, Jesus arose.

He arose the victor of the dark domain, and He lives forever with His saints to reign. He arose! He arose! Hallelujah! Christ arose!

CHAPTER 6

HE AROSE

The resurrection of Jesus was the greatest event in the history of the world. Our entire salvation is dependent on this single event. If Jesus were still dead, then we wouldn't be forgiven. First Corinthians 15:16-17 says, "For if the dead do not rise, then Christ is not risen. And if Christ is not risen, your faith is futile; you are still in your sins!" But here's the Good News. Jesus is alive. We go to church because He arose from the dead. We sing songs and have hope for the future because He arose. We have Good News to share and a good life to live because Jesus lives, and heaven is awaiting our arrival because of His resurrection.

Everything we believe in the New Testament hinges on this powerful moment, so let's take a closer look at the resurrection of Jesus.

Let's begin with Matthew's account.

> *Now after the Sabbath, as the first day of the week began to dawn, Mary Magdalene and the other Mary came to see the tomb. And behold, there was a great earthquake; for an*

angel of the Lord descended from heaven, and came and rolled back the stone from the door, and sat on it. His countenance was like lightning, and his clothing as white as snow. And the guards shook for fear of him, and became like dead men. But the angel answered and said to the women, "Do not be afraid, for I know that you seek Jesus who was crucified. He is not here; for He is risen, as He said. Come, see the place where the Lord lay. And go quickly and tell His disciples that He is risen from the dead, and indeed He is going before you into Galilee; there you will see Him. Behold, I have told you." So they went out quickly from the tomb with fear and great joy, and ran to bring His disciples word.

—Matthew 28:1-8

> "There is no single event on the earth as important as the resurrection."

His disciples have been bringing this word to people ever since. There is no single event on the earth as important as the resurrection. Tourists visit an empty tomb in Jerusalem because He is risen.

But notice what Paul said about our preaching.

And if Christ is not risen, then our preaching is empty and your faith is also empty.

1 Corinthians 15:14

Paul was telling us if Christ were not risen, then redemption did not work. We would still be in sin and unforgiven. If this were true, there would be no Good News. Romans 4:25 says it this way, "who was delivered up because of our offenses, and was raised because of our justification."

In other words, if Jesus died for our sins and He was still dead, then the price would not have been paid. But if Jesus is alive, then He was raised for our justification. When we were forgiven and justified, the price was paid, and Jesus was raised from the dead.

This price was paid for all mankind, but Romans 10 tells us how we receive salvation.

> *That if you confess with your mouth the Lord Jesus and believe in your heart that God has raised Him from the dead, you will be saved. For with the heart one believes unto righteousness, and with the mouth confession is made unto salvation.*
>
> —Romans 10:9-10

So in order to receive salvation, we must confess Jesus as Lord and believe God raised Him from the dead. You can believe He was given by God and born of a virgin. You can believe He lived on the earth and was fully God and fully man. You can believe He lived a sinless life and performed miracles while He was here, but to be saved, you have to believe in the resurrection.

If Jesus is alive, all is well, but if He's dead there is no hope. There would be no reason to sing if He's not alive.

There would be no future for us if He's not alive. There would be no escape from sin and death if He's not alive.

Life would have no meaning if there was no resurrection.

Let's look again at the words of Paul in the New Living Translation.

> *And if Christ has not been raised, then your faith is useless and you are still guilty of your sins. In that case, all who have died believing in Christ are lost! And if our hope in Christ is only for this life, we are more to be pitied than anyone in the world.*

—1 Corinthians 15:17-19 (NLT)

Easter is not just the celebration of a mythical bunny and brightly colored eggs. It's a time to remember and celebrate the resurrection of Jesus. If there is just one truth the world needs to know, it's that Jesus—our Savior—was raised from the dead. Let's make sure we take the opportunity to let the world know what Easter is all about. I'm certainly not opposed to Easter egg hunts and some of the other traditions we practice every year during this special holiday. Many churches have used these events to tell children and

> "If there is just one truth the world needs to know, it's that Jesus—our Savior—was raised from the dead."

parents the true meaning of Easter. We should take advantage of every opportunity to share the gospel. The Easter holiday provides a wonderful opportunity to tell people that God raised Jesus from the dead.

It's the best news that's ever been told. When Jesus arose from the dead, He defeated the devil. He triumphed over the evil one. Satan had no idea that the crucifixion and death of Jesus would break his power over mankind and provide salvation for the lost. This was a mystery hidden from the foundation of the world (Romans 16:25). The work of the cross was God's hidden plan, which was kept secret until after the resurrection.

> But we speak the wisdom of God in a mystery, the hidden wisdom which God ordained before the ages for our glory, which none of the rulers of this age knew; for had they known, they would not have crucified the Lord of glory.
>
> —1 Corinthians 2:7-8

Satan and his kingdom were behind the politics that sent Jesus to the cross. He so influenced the people of that day that He compelled them to crucify an innocent man. Not only was Jesus innocent of breaking any laws, but also He was the only Man who had never sinned. Satan stirred such hatred in the hearts of His accusers that they crucified the one Man who had a right to live.

The apostles' prayer in Acts 4 reveals how God used the ungodly to further His divine purposes in the earth.

> *"For truly against Your holy Servant Jesus, whom You anointed, both Herod and Pontius Pilate, with the Gentiles and the people of Israel, were gathered together to do whatever Your hand and Your purpose determined before to be done."*
>
> —Acts 4:27-28

The Jews and the Gentiles came together to stand against Jesus. They were inspired by the devil to kill Him. Yet, in their haste to rid the world of Jesus, they facilitated God's plan for our redemption. It doesn't pay to work against God. He has ways and means to accomplish His plans that are beyond the imagination.

When Jesus arose, the power of Satan over mankind was forever broken, and a new day of freedom and liberty had begun.

> *Having disarmed principalities and powers, He made a public spectacle of them, triumphing over them in it.*
>
> —Colossians 2:15

Jesus defeated our enemy and gave us the victory.

Notice how the following translations of Colossians 2:15 describe this spectacular event.

> *"...having spoiled principalities and powers..."*
>
> —KJV

> *"...He disarmed [stripped off] the spiritual rulers and authorities. He shamed them publicly by his victory over them on the cross."*
>
> —NLT (brackets mine)

Then look at Hebrews 2.

> *...through death He might destroy him who had the power of death, that is, the devil, and release those who through fear of death were all their lifetime subject to bondage.*
>
> —Hebrews 2:14-15

We don't know all the details of this spectacular event, but we do know the devil is now a defeated foe through Jesus Christ. He never even saw it coming.

> *He has delivered us from the power of darkness and conveyed us into the kingdom of the Son of His love.*
>
> —Colossians 1:13

It's important to note once again that Jesus was a man. He was born of a woman, though He was fully God and fully man all at the same time. A man yielded to the enemy's temptations and put all men under Satan's dominion on resurrection day, but the Man defeated the devil. Jesus—our representative Man—defeated the devil on our behalf. The second Adam got back what the first Adam lost.

We think in these terms often. For example, we say man discovered electricity or man invented the airplane or man invented the polio vaccine. When one man breaks through certain barriers, all men benefit. In the same way, we can now say man defeated the devil. Man overcame death, and a man is seated at the right hand of God. We made it!

About to be stoned, Stephen gives us an eyewitness account of what he saw in heaven. Jesus was seated at the right hand of God but stood up for Stephen's entrance.

> *But he, being full of the Holy Spirit, gazed into heaven and saw the glory of God, and Jesus standing at the right hand of God, and said, "Look! I see the heavens opened and the Son of Man standing at the right hand of God!"*
>
> —Acts 7:55-56

Jesus is one of us. He will forever be a man. The Man, Christ Jesus. He became one with us so He could lift us up that we might be seated with Him in heavenly places. Not only has man walked on the moon, but through Jesus, man has ascended to the right hand of God. We will forever enjoy this place beside the Father through our Lord Jesus Christ.

Jesus prayed for all of us before His death, and this prayer is recorded in John 17. This is one of the most heart-felt, revealing prayers recorded in scripture. Two things are obvious in this prayer: One is that Jesus was in love with the Father, and the other is that He was in love with people. Let's look at one verse from this amazing prayer.

> *"Father, I desire that they also whom You gave Me may be with Me where I am, that they may behold My glory which You have given Me; for You loved Me before the foundation of the world."*
>
> —John 17:24

Jesus laid aside His glory to become a man and to live on the earth as a human being. No one can imagine what a sacrifice that was. One of His great desires was that we could see Him as He is in all of His glory. And one day, we will.

John saw the resurrected Christ and wrote about it in the book of Revelation. John had been Jesus' friend, and they were so close the Bible identifies John as the disciple whom Jesus loved. But even John was not prepared to see Jesus in His glory after the resurrection. He tells us that one look at Him and he fell at His feet as a dead man.

Let's look at John's description of the resurrected Christ.

> *And standing in the middle of the lampstands was someone like the Son of Man. He was wearing a long robe with a gold sash across his chest. His head and his hair were white like wool, as white as snow. And his eyes were like flames of fire. His feet were like polished bronze refined in a furnace, and his voice thundered like mighty ocean waves. He held seven stars in his right hand, and a sharp*

two-edged sword came from his mouth. And his face was like the sun in all its brilliance. When I saw him, I fell at his feet as if I were dead. But he laid his right hand on me and said, "Don't be afraid! I am the First and the Last. I am the living one. I died, but look—I am alive forever and ever! And I hold the keys of death and the grave."

—Revelation 1:13-18 (NLT)

Jesus is alive and glorified, and He has the keys. The keys represent authority, and Jesus took them back from Satan who had taken them from Adam. A man lost our authority, and the Man got it back. Jesus did for us what we could never do for ourselves. He defeated our greatest enemies—sin, sickness, disease, death and the devil. That's why we have Good News to preach today. Jesus did the work, and we get the benefits. All that is left to do about sin and death is to tell the world what Jesus has done, and let the whole world know that Jesus is not dead. Jesus is alive forevermore, and the Good News just can't get any better than that.

CHAPTER 7

JESUS

There is no one like Jesus. We could talk about Him for days or weeks at a time and attempt to describe who He is to the best of our ability, and Jesus would still be a thousand times greater than we could ever express or comprehend. We see through a glass darkly while we live on this earth, and we do the best we can. It will take the clarity of heaven and the space of eternity to truly appreciate who He is and all He is. The apostle Paul prayed that we "may be able to comprehend with all the saints what is the width and length and depth and height—to know the love of Christ which passes knowledge...." (Ephesians 3:18)

Jesus is the most important person in the entire universe, and these verses written about Him in Colossians help us understand His role in creation.

> *He is the image of the invisible God, the firstborn over all creation. For by Him all things were created that are in heaven and that are on earth, visible and invisible, whether thrones or dominions or*

> *principalities or powers. All things were*
> *created through Him and for Him. And He*
> *is before all things, and in Him all things*
> *consist.*
>
> —Colossians 1:15-17

We see clearly that Jesus is at the center of everything that is made. Let's look at verses 16 and 17, and see how it reads by replacing the words *Him* and *He* with the name *Jesus.*

All things were created through Jesus and for Jesus, and Jesus is before all things and in Jesus all things consist (are upheld or held together).

John makes a similar point about Jesus in his gospel:

> *In the beginning was the Word, and the Word*
> *was with God, and the Word was God. He*
> *was in the beginning with God. All things*
> *were made through Him, and without Him*
> *nothing was made that was made.*
>
> —John 1:1-3

We know *the Word* that John is talking about is Jesus because in John 1:14 he says, "And the Word became flesh and dwelt among us...."

Now, let's put the name of Jesus in the first three verses of John 1 where John is speaking of Him.

1 In the beginning was Jesus, and Jesus was with God, and Jesus was God.

2 Jesus was in the beginning with God.

3 All things were made through Jesus and without Jesus nothing was made that was made.

These verses and many others in the Bible relay what an important place Jesus fills in creation. It was all made with Him, by Him, for Him, and even now, He holds it all together. Yet, no one has been more ignored, overlooked and blasphemed than Jesus.

According to the scriptures, we read that Jesus had a central role in creation from the very beginning. He was there. We know that God has eternally existed as a triune being—Father, Son and Holy Ghost. So Jesus was present, although not mentioned by name in the book of Genesis. What was His role? As we shall see, it was the same then as it is today, Savior and Lord.

The act of creation was an act of love. The Father's heart yearned for children. As we discussed earlier, planet Earth is where the Father chose to raise His family, and it's no accident that the earth is the only planet with the necessary conditions to sustain life.

"God chose us, and He wanted us to have the right to choose Him."

That's exactly why God created it. It is our present home, and it's the place where humans are born and become aware of their own existence. It was designed to be the place where people are educated and discover their own identity. This journey into self-awareness on the earth is supposed to lead people on a search for God and result in finding Him and entering into a personal relationship with Him. God designed the earth to be the place where His family could become a reality.

God wanted His family to be made up of people as much like God as He could make them—His very offspring. In order to do this and enjoy the highest level of fellowship possible, God had to give them a free will or the ability to choose. They couldn't be robots or preprogramed beings who automatically worshipped God. Their love had to be real, and their worship had to come from the heart. The greatest love that can be experienced is when two people who have the ability to choose whomever they want, choose each other.

God chose us, and He wanted us to have the right to choose Him.

Yet, God knows everything. He knows the end from the beginning. So before anything was made, God knew that if He made man in His image and gave Him a free will, man would sin. He knew man would choose death in the garden. He knew this before there was a garden. God, being a good God, would never have gone forward with the act of creation knowing that mankind would die in sin.

I believe that sometime back in eternity past, before time or the world existed, God had a dream for a family. He dreamed of you and me. When the thought of creation was conceived in the mind of God, He knew that man would sin and creation would be destroyed. He knew that the result of sin was that man would perish and be eternally separated from God. So, at some point in this process, the decision was made that Jesus would be the Savior.

As God's plans for His family were being conceived and the dream of God was being formed, at just the right moment, Jesus stepped forward and said, "Father, make the world just as You've dreamed. Make man in Our image and after Our likeness, and give him the ability to choose. I know mankind will sin, and I know creation will be destroyed as the result of sin, but I will go and pay for it. I will become one of them. I will take their place. I will suffer for them, and I will pay the price to buy them back. You make it, and I will pay for it." God accepted His offer because of His great love for us. At that moment, God became the Father who gave His only begotten Son. Jesus became the Savior, and the plan of salvation we preach today was born.

The plan was in motion before the world was made. Jesus became the lamb slain from the foundation of the world. He became our Savior, our answer, our redeemer. There wouldn't be a world without Jesus. God would have never made the world just to send its inhabitants to hell. Without a Savior there would be no creation. There would be no cities or nations. There would be no trees or animals. There would be nothing to sing about, no future to enjoy. We would not exist.

Everything that is, owes its existence to Jesus Christ. Even sinners who take His name in vain and seem not to care whether there is a God or not, would not exist without Him. Every square foot of ground they walk on, every breath they take, was made possible by Jesus. All things were created by Jesus and for Jesus.

No one in this world is more important or more worthy of honor and adoration than Jesus Christ. We could spend weeks and even months living in our own nation and never hear His name mentioned unless it's being used as a curse word. But don't think for a single minute that because Jesus is ignored and overlooked that He isn't all the Bible says He is. Jesus is the King of Kings and the Lord of Lords. He is the way, the truth and the life. No man comes to the Father except by Him. That was the plan from the beginning—even before the beginning—and it's the plan today. It is all because of Jesus. One day, every knee will bow, and every tongue will confess that Jesus Christ is Lord.

Jesus is the first and the last, the beginning and the end. There will be many people, nations, religions and philosophies who will make their voices heard. But make no mistake. Jesus is the beginning and the end. He had the first word, and He will have the last word. It's not up to North Korea, China, Russia or the USA to decide when this world comes to an end. Revelation 21:6 tells us that Jesus will let us all know when He's finished (NLT), and it's not finished until He says it is.

When it is finished, the Father will gather His family, and He will spend all of eternity showing forth what He will do for those He loves. His dream will come true as it has been mentioned throughout His Word through prophecies and promises.

We are one family—God the Father and His sons and daughters. Jesus is our Savior forever; we are joined to Him, and He is joined to us. Those of us who have received Jesus will have a special relationship with Him forever. He will always be our Savior, our Master, our Redeemer and our Lord. He in us, and we in Him. Our union with Him is beyond our understanding, and yet, it is true. It is real, and it is eternal.

Scientists have been searching for decades for what they call "the missing link," which is a fossil or bone or some physical evidence proving a link between man and animals—perhaps an earlier version of "Neanderthal man." They have not been able to find it, and I'll tell you why. There is no link between man and animals. Man is not an animal and never was.

Notice what 1 Timothy says.

> *For there is one God and one Mediator between God and men, the Man Christ Jesus.*
>
> —1 Timothy 2:5

The missing link is Jesus. He doesn't link man to animals; He links man to God. We are the offspring of God Himself through Jesus Christ. Jesus made us one with Himself. We are heirs of God and joint heirs with Jesus. He has lifted us up and raised us up and seated us with Him in heavenly places (Ephesians 2:6).

God did something about all the sin and evil that exists in the world. He provided an answer. He sent us a Savior, and His name is Jesus. He is the way, the truth and the life.

No one else could have done for us what Jesus did, and if they could have, they probably wouldn't have. Yet, He did. Jesus is the rightful King of all the earth. There is no other like Him. We can never repay Him for what He has done for us, and He doesn't expect us to. But we can be grateful, and we can help spread the Good News around the world.

GOOD NEWS

It's not my job to censor other voices or silence other messages. I don't even want to. That would violate the free will others have been given as a gift from God. But at the very least, we should give Jesus equal time.

> "There is nothing this world needs more today than an encounter with the Savior, Jesus Christ."

Pastor John Osteen from Houston, Texas, told about an experience he had along these lines. He was taking care of business in a public building in Houston one day, and when he got on the elevator, several men were talking and cursing. In Texas vernacular, Brother Osteen said, "They were cussing a blue streak!" There really isn't time on an elevator to preach a sermon or have a discussion about the virtues of clean speech. So, rather than get into an argument, the pastor lifted both hands and said, "Hallelujah! Thank You, Jesus!" The men instantly got quiet and looked at Brother Osteen, as if waiting for an explanation for this sudden outburst of religious fanaticism. Think about it. Cursing God in public is routine and a perfectly acceptable way to express oneself, but if you praise God in public, you need to give an explanation. Brother Osteen didn't hesitate, he answered by saying, "I'm just trying to give Jesus equal time!"

That is a wonderful attitude. It's not our job to get everyone we disagree with to stop talking. It's our job to give Jesus equal time. We have the best message in the world, and it is important that we do our best to get the word out.

There is nothing that compares to the message of Jesus Christ—nothing else even comes close. The more you get to know Him, the more beautiful and wonderful you realize He is. We must let the world know who Jesus is. May God's Holy Spirit help us put Jesus back into the national dialogue. There is nothing this world needs more today than an encounter with the Savior, Jesus Christ.

CHAPTER 8

FORGIVENESS:

A PRELUDE TO RIGHTEOUSNESS

Forgiveness is one of the most important doctrines in the Bible. God was serious about forgiveness, and Jesus paid a high price to provide it. He served the ultimate purpose and paid the ultimate price to purchase you back from the penalties of sin. When the angel of the Lord appeared to Joseph, He said "...you shall call His name Jesus, for He will save His people from their sins" (Matthew 1:21).

The book of Hebrews teaches us much about the subject of forgiveness. In Hebrews 9 and 10, the writer of Hebrews compares what the Old Covenant sacrifices accomplished for God's people in those days to what Jesus has done for us today in the New Covenant. Under the Old Covenant, the blood of bulls and goats was brought into the tabernacle and offered as a covering for the sins of the people. This was done once every year by the high priest and served only to cover sins—not remove them.

*For the law, having a shadow of the good
things to come, and not the very image of the
things, can never with these same sacrifices,
which they offer continually year by year,
make those who approach perfect. For then
would they not have ceased to be offered? For
the worshipers, once purified, would have
had no more consciousness of sins.*

—Hebrews 10:1-2

This was the best they could hope for until the true
sacrifice came to make an offering for sins, once and for
all. If this Old Testament method had been sufficient to
forgive sins, it would not have had to be repeated every
year.

*But in those sacrifices there is a reminder of
sins every year. For it is not possible that the
blood of bulls and goats could take away sins.*

—Hebrews 10:3-4

Animal sacrifices were never intended to be the final
solution to the sin problem. Jesus is the true sacrifice
for sins, and the teaching in Hebrews makes a great
distinction between Jesus' blood and the blood of animals
offered in the tabernacle. The blood of animals used to
cover the sins of the people was offered countless times
by the high priest over the years.

What Jesus did was sufficient to forgive sins
forever. Consequently, He only had to do it one time.
The words *one* and *once* are used seven times in Hebrews
9 and 10.

Let's look at two instances of their use in Hebrews 9:

> *He then would have had to suffer often since the foundation of the world; but now, once at the end of the ages, He has appeared to put away sin by the sacrifice of Himself.*
>
> —Hebrews 9:26

> *So Christ was offered once to bear the sins of many. To those who eagerly wait for Him He will appear a second time, apart from sin, for salvation.*
>
> —Hebrews 9:28

The word *once* has great significance as it pertains to forgiveness. Jesus only had to pay the price for sin one time. One time was enough to settle the sin debt.

Jesus came to set us free from sin. He died on the cross, and at some point after the resurrection, He ascended to the true Holy of Holies before the very throne of God in heaven. He offered His holy, spotless blood to the Father as payment for our sins. We get a glimpse of this wonderful event when Jesus appeared to Mary Magdalene just after His resurrection.

> *Jesus saith unto her, Touch me not; for I am not yet ascended to my Father: but go to my brethren, and say unto them, I ascend unto my Father, and your Father; and to my God, and your God.*
>
> —John 20:17 (KJV)

Most Bible scholars believe that this is the point at which Jesus took His blood and offered it as an eternal atonement for sin. He had already defeated Satan, and He was ascending to the Father to present His blood in the Holy of Holies. This was the ultimate payment necessary for our forgiveness.

Notice the following verses in Hebrews 10.

> *By that will we have been sanctified through the offering of the body of Jesus Christ once for all. And every priest stands ministering daily and offering repeatedly the same sacrifices, which can never take away sins. But this Man, after He had offered one sacrifice for sins forever, sat down at the right hand of God, from that time waiting till His enemies are made His footstool. For by one offering He has perfected forever those who are being sanctified.*

> —Hebrews 10:10-14

In addition to the words *one* and *once*, these verses add the words *for all* and *forever.* What this means to us is that what Jesus did over two thousand years ago has forgiven us all—forever. He offered one sacrifice— for all sins—forever. There will never have to be another payment. Jesus' blood was enough.

> *then He adds, "Their sins and their lawless deeds I will remember no more." Now where there is remission of these, there is no longer an offering for sin.*

> —Hebrews 10:17-18

Hebrews tells us, not only are sins forgiven, but also forgotten. God does not remember them anymore. That means when you approach God in prayer, He's not going to remind you of your past mistakes; so you shouldn't spend your time reminding Him. He has forgiven and forgotten them. There is no use in digging them back up and living in the past.

Along with the sin came guilt and condemnation. Let it go! You must accept the teaching in Hebrews about forgiveness and accept forgiveness for your own sins. This is not a doctrine for everyone else. It is for *you*. Some people need help accepting God's forgiveness.

> "When you continue to feel guilty over past sins and try to pay for them with your own emotions or actions, you're not accepting what Jesus did as full payment."

Now, I'm in no way diminishing the awfulness of sin. It's bad. It's even worse than we know. However, the value of the blood of Jesus is greater than we could have ever dreamed. It is the blood that forgives and the incomprehensible value of His blood that paid our debt. God accepted it as payment for all sins for all time.

When you continue to feel guilty over past sins and try to pay for them with your own emotions or actions, you're not accepting what Jesus did as full payment. You can never add to what He did. He paid the price in full.

85

Your suffering doesn't add to what He did. It doesn't count at all.

Hebrews 10:18 says, "Now where there is remission of these, there is no longer an offering for sin." There is no longer an offering for sin because it's already been paid. It's time to move on. Don't ever think that out of all the people who have ever sinned, you have committed the one sin Jesus cannot forgive. Not so. Don't flatter yourself. His blood was enough even for your worst sins. It's not the power of your sin or the result of your mistakes that remains; it's the power of His blood that overcomes. No amount of grieving, tears or sadness can add to what He's done for you. You cannot punish yourself to help Him pay for your sins.

When memories of past sins return to condemn you with feelings of guilt and condemnation, remember what Jesus did for you. Count on the value of His blood to forgive, save and redeem you.

> How much more shall the blood of Christ, who through the eternal Spirit offered Himself without spot to God, cleanse your conscience from dead works to serve the living God?
>
> —Hebrews 9:14

Guilt and sins can stain your conscience, and the result is ongoing condemnation. It is possible to have a guilty conscience concerning some sin God has already forgiven. This is what John is speaking of in 1 John 3:20, "For if our heart condemns us, God is greater than our heart, and knows all things."

Apply faith in His blood, and let that cleanse your conscience from guilt. Don't let the enemy rob you of your time with God or your sense of acceptance and forgiveness. God has forgiven you of all your sins if you have accepted Jesus as Lord. It's important that you realize that forgiveness isn't a feeling; it's a fact. Accept God's Word on the matter—not what you feel. Forgiveness, like many other benefits in the New Testament, is received by faith.

Some people can accept forgiveness for "small" sins, but not for "big" sins. The truth is, either Jesus forgave you of all your sins or He hasn't forgiven you for any sins. Many Christians are robbed of their fellowship with God because they allow guilt and condemnation to get in the way. If they would only believe in the doctrine of forgiveness, they could let go of the past and run into the future unhindered by the memories of past mistakes.

> *Having wiped out the handwriting of requirements that was against us, which was contrary to us. And He has taken it out of the way, having nailed it to the cross.*
>
> —Colossians 2:14

God has removed any record of your past sins. Let's look at a couple of modern translations of Colossians 2:14:

> *God crossed out the whole debt against us in His account books. He no longer counted the*

laws we had broken. He nailed the account book to the cross and closed the account.

—Laubach

He destroyed the record of the debts standing against us...He nailed it to the cross and put it out of sight.

—Plain English Bible

Whatever records there were in heaven documenting your sins have been destroyed. They no longer exist. Let guilt and condemnation go with them, and enjoy a life of fellowship with God the Father.

Who shall bring a charge against God's elect? It is God who justifies. Who is he who condemns? It is Christ who died, and furthermore is also risen, who is even at the right hand of God, who also makes intercession for us.

—Romans 8:33-34

If you are dealing with guilt from past mistakes, where is it coming from? Not from God. He is the One who justified you. Who is condemning you? Not Jesus. He paid a high price for your freedom. Does it really matter what anyone else thinks? Is it Satan who is reminding you of your guilt? Is it your friends or relatives who won't let you forget the past? Maybe your mind is your own worst enemy.

Look at this paraphrase of Romans 8.

We are the people of His covenant, citizens of His charter, sons of His compassion. Let the accuser launch his charges. They will fall harmless to the ground. The judge of all the world has set our feet upon the way of righteousness. There is no other court that can reverse that verdict. Think of Christ crucified...And remember that the crucified is now risen. He is now seated at the right hand of the majesty on High. It is His voice that says all the time, "Father, remember those for whom I died." That precious death, that mighty resurrection, that glorious ascension, that good shepherdly pleading at the right hand of God, that marvelous series of creative acts, has forged a union that cannot be broken. The love of Christ has gathered us, and no power, save that of our own defiant will, can tear us from His keeping.

—Romans 8:33-34 (Carpenter)

Our case has already been tried by the Supreme Court of the universe, and we have been declared not guilty. No other court can change that verdict. We are now free to enjoy access to God that only a son or daughter can enjoy with no sense of guilt or shame.

It's as if the writer of Hebrews was climbing a mountain from Hebrews chapter one to chapter 10. When he gets to chapter 10, he finally reaches the summit. After comparing the sacrifices in the Old Testament with the redemptive work of Christ in the New Testament, the writer of Hebrews reveals the reason for our redemption. We see God's dream for His children fulfilled after centuries of sin and separation.

> *Therefore, brethren, having boldness to enter the Holiest by the blood of Jesus, by a new and living way which He consecrated for us, through the veil, that is, His flesh, and having a High Priest over the house of God.*
>
> —Hebrews 10:19-21

"We belong in His presence with no guilt, no fear and no condemnation."

Hebrews 10:19 begins with the word *therefore*, and it's important. It means that all the sacrifices from Moses and the Old Testament tabernacle to Jesus and the cross and the shedding of His blood have led us to this conclusion: We have boldness to enter into the Holiest. There are many places on the earth that people may consider holy, but there is only one place that is the Holiest. That is the very presence of God. Angels fear to tread there. Man had not been allowed there since the garden of Eden, but now, through the new and living way, we have entrance into the Holiest. This is what it's been about from the beginning. This was God's dream, and now it's a reality. We can go into the holiest place—the throne room of God—with boldness. It's as if the entire Bible leads us to this one single point. It's a place of freedom to fellowship with God.

In fact, *you* have been given a divine invitation:

> *Let us draw near with a true heart in full assurance of faith, having our hearts sprinkled from an evil conscience and our bodies washed with pure water.*
>
> —Hebrews 10:22

So, let us draw near. If we get all our doctrine right, all our theology sound, and we are experts in all the principles of the kingdom but miss this, we've missed the whole point. We must draw near—near to the throne, near to the presence of God, near to the heart of God. This was His dream. It's why you and I and every human being was born. This is where all the teaching on forgiveness and redemption takes on real meaning. We belong in His presence with no guilt, no fear and no condemnation. It's from this place our prayers work, our fellowship with the Father is real and our life springs from our time with Him.

> *Beloved, if our heart does not condemn us, we have confidence toward God. And whatever we ask we receive from Him, because we keep His commandments and do those things that are pleasing in His sight.*
>
> —1 John 3:21-22

It's the forgiven souls who are confident in who they are and what they have in Christ, and who are ready to enter in and enjoy a happy, healthy relationship with the Father. These individuals accept the fact of their forgiveness through faith in God's Word. It is when faith in God's Word ascends above feelings, the heart is free from condemnation, and confidence prevails. This is when faith in God soars, and prayers are effective. This is the right of every born-again believer, and it was all made possible by Jesus and His marvelous work of redemption.

CHAPTER 9

A NEW IDENTITY

Our spiritual condition inherited from Adam was unacceptable. We were sinners because of his transgression. Ephesians 2:1 says we were dead in trespasses and sin. In other words, we were separated from God and unfit to enter His presence. We were beyond rehabilitation. It was impossible for us to work our way out of this sinful state. Sin was not just something we had done; it was who we were. Something radical had to be done if we were to ever take our place in God's presence. In fact, something as radical as death itself was required to fix the problem. The only solution was death. *We had to die.*

It is futile for any descendant of Adam to try to work his or her way to God. No matter how hard one works or how much they sacrifice, human efforts cannot change the sin nature. The sin nature in the heart of man is at enmity with God.

Romans 6:23 says, "For the wages of sin is death…", and sin and the sin nature made us worthy of death. From the time of Adam's sin onward, all of humanity lived with a death sentence hanging over our heads. We were "by nature the children of wrath," Ephesians 2:3 says. Our nature was inherited from our father Adam and could not be changed, no matter how hard we tried. It was sinful and unrighteous. It was who we were, and it had to go.

Here's the simple truth. Forgiveness can release one from the liability of committed sins, but only death can deliver one from the sin nature that was passed down to every human from Adam.

We have looked at the law of substitution and learned how Jesus died for us, but let's consider the law of identification. This action takes our union with Christ a step further. Not only did Jesus die for us, but if we accept Him and become one with Him, we can say we died in Him. This was God's method of providing death for our deliverance without annihilating us in the process.

> *For the love of Christ compels us, because we judge thus: that if One died for all, then all died.*
>
> —2 Corinthians 5:14

Not only did Jesus die for us, but we died *in Him*. This is an important point to consider. We needed to die because of sin, but death is such a final outcome. How could God's dream for a family come to pass if we all died? Miraculously enough, God accomplished our death for sin through the work of His son. Through the law of identification, we died in Him. Legally in the eyes of God and for all time, we died in Christ.

There are several scriptures that take us through every step of this process. They are a powerful witness to the fact that in Christ, you died and are now free from sin, free from the old man you used to be. The scriptures also testify to the fact that you have received new life. Jesus didn't simply and only die; He was raised from the dead. We became one with Him by faith in Him. We died with Him, and we were also raised to live new life with Him. Death did not have the final say. It was followed by a glorious resurrection and a new life in God.

Let's look at what the Word of God has to say on the subject of our identification with Christ. When we accepted Jesus as Lord, we became one with Him. Not only did He die for us, but we also died in Him. He died by crucifixion, so the scriptures show our participation with Him from this point forward.

> *I have been crucified with Christ; it is no longer I who live, but Christ lives in me; and the life which I now live in the flesh I live by faith in the Son of God, who loved me and gave Himself for me.*
>
> —Galatians 2:20

> *Knowing this, that our old man was crucified with Him, that the body of sin might be done away with, that we should no longer be slaves of sin.*
>
> —Romans 6:6

> *But God forbid that I should boast except in the cross of our Lord Jesus Christ, by whom*

> *the world has been crucified to me, and I to*
> *the world.*
>
> —Galatians 6:14

It is liberating to say aloud, *I was crucified with Him!*
When He died, I died! Especially if you're dealing with
guilt and memories of failure from your past, you can say
along with the apostle Paul, *I was crucified with Christ!*

Once again, our death with Christ is mentioned in 2
Corinthians 5.

> *For the love of Christ compels us, because we*
> *judge thus: that if One died for all, then all*
> *died.*
>
> —2 Corinthians 5:14

Listen to yourself as you say aloud, *I was crucified with*
Him, and I died with Him.

Now let's look at two more references dealing with
our death with Him:

> *Who Himself bore our sins in His own body*
> *on the tree, that we, having died to sins,*
> *might live for righteousness....*
>
> —1 Peter 2:24

> *For you died, and your life is hidden with*
> *Christ in God.*
>
> —Colossians 3:3

Remember, for the sinner, death is a necessity. You were a sinner. You could not be rehabilitated. You had to die, and the old man you used to be *has died*. You were crucified with Jesus. You died with Him, and then you were buried with Him.

> *Buried with Him in baptism, in which you also were raised with Him through faith in the working of God, who raised Him from the dead.*
>
> —Colossians 2:12

We are crucified with Christ. We were buried with Him and then raised to new life with Him. His death was our death, and therefore, His resurrection was our resurrection. Death alone would have been a failure. It would have robbed God of His family and eternally separated us from Him. Death in Christ, however,

> "Death in Christ released us from the past and allowed us to be reborn with a new nature—the nature of God Himself."

released us from the past and allowed us to be reborn with a new nature—the nature of God Himself.

> *Therefore we were buried with Him through baptism into death, that just as Christ was raised from the dead by the glory of the Father, even so we also should walk in newness of life.*
>
> —Romans 6:4

Your old sin loving nature was buried with Him in baptism when He died, and when God the Father, with glorious power, brought Him back to life again, you were given His wonderful new life to enjoy.

—Romans 6:4 (Taylor)

When Jesus was made alive, we were made alive with Him.

And you, being dead in your trespasses and the uncircumcision of your flesh, He has made alive together with Him, having forgiven you all trespasses.

—Colossians 2:13

God breathed into us the very life of Christ.

Even when we were dead in trespasses, made us alive together with Christ (by grace you have been saved).

—Ephesians 2:5

Then, when He was raised, we were raised with Him.

And raised us up together, and made us sit together in the heavenly places in Christ Jesus.

—Ephesians 2:6

If then you were raised with Christ, seek those things which are above, where Christ is, sitting at the right hand of God.

—Colossians 3:1

We are seated with Jesus in a place of authority. We went from outcasts to the very right hand of God. We went from the lowest place to the highest place, and now we enjoy a place of authority and favor with God.

Jesus endured the sufferings of Calvary for us. When we accepted Him, we joined Him in this process of death, burial and resurrection. It became personal. Not only did Christ die for me, but also, I died in Him. In Him, I was raised to new life.

Jesus used an ingenious term to communicate this total transformation when talking to Nicodemus (John 3). He simply said, "You must be born again." Nothing can describe the changes that happened to us in our union with Christ like the words *born again* or *new birth*. Jesus made the complex understandable with simple words and plain language by saying, "You must be born again."

Nicodemus replied with a question, "How can a man be born when he is old?" Naturally speaking, it's impossible. Yet, God did the impossible for us through Jesus Christ. Our union with Christ in His death, burial, resurrection and ascension makes the impossible possible for us who believe.

Notice how this is expressed in 2 Corinthians 5:17, "Therefore, if anyone is in Christ, he is a new creation; old things have passed away; behold, all things have become new."

I have passed away. The old sinful person I was has died.

If you call Jesus, Lord, then you have passed away. Your old sinful person has died.

This is a powerful scripture revealing a powerful truth. Something died, and someone new came into being at the new birth.

We are new creations—a new species of being that never before existed.

All of these things occur inside the human heart at the time of salvation, though they are invisible. It takes revelation knowledge and an understanding of the redemptive scriptures in the Epistles to truly grasp the significance of the new birth. These are truths that will set you free.

It is very liberating to know and understand that the old you was crucified with Christ, and now you live. It's not the old you that lives, but a new you. You have been raised and seated with Christ. You have a new nature that is acceptable to God. It is helpful to speak these new creation realities to yourself, and allow them to renew or reprogram your mind. Christ has given you a new identity, and being continually aware of this will change your life. You are no longer bound to the past and limited by what the old man has done. The old man you were is dead. Period. End of story. You are a new creation with the nature of God on the inside.

> *Likewise you also, reckon yourselves to be*
> *dead indeed to sin, but alive to God in Christ*

Jesus our Lord.

—Romans 6:11

Even though the new birth is real—and it really happened to you and in you—it's helpful to reckon it to be so. Jesus wanted us to understand the radical changes that occurred on the inside when we were saved. One of the first acts of worship we are commanded to do by the Lord after salvation is to follow Him in water baptism. This is a physical reenactment of that which happened to your spirit in Christ when you were born again. It is a living picture of your death with Him, your burial and your being raised up with Him to new life. It is so simple, yet so powerful. Every time we see a Christian being water baptized, he or she is going through outward steps to gain a better understanding of what happened on the inside.

Nevertheless, one of the most effective ways to get the wonderful truths on the inside of us working on the outside of us is to speak them. This is essential if we are going to "put on the new man" as Paul tells us to do in Ephesians 4:24. We can see the significance of speaking the Word in this next verse:

> *That the sharing of your faith may become effective by the acknowledgment of every good thing which is in you in Christ Jesus.*
>
> —Philemon 1:6

Take time to say who you are and what you have in Him. This information is not readily available in the world around you. It can only be found in the Epistles. It's very easy to forget what God has done in your spirit and, therefore, not experience the benefits that are yours now in Christ. James compares this to a man looking at himself in a mirror then walking away and forgetting what he looked like (James 1:23).

Many years ago, I took a notebook and wrote down every scripture I could find that had to do with my new identity in Christ. I wrote down almost every verse in Paul's Epistles that contained the words *in Christ, in Him and in whom.* I wore out the paper as I carried it with me and read out loud all that I had and all that I was in Christ. This had a life-changing effect on me. I've never been the same since. It changed my thinking and my speech, and it will do the same for any Christian. I highly recommend you try this for yourself.

Don't wait for other people to confirm who you are, and don't look to the world for approval. Become acquainted with who you are in Christ. You will only get this information from God's Word. Take time to meditate on scriptures that tell you who you are and what you have in Christ. Look for the verses in the Epistles that include the phrases *in Christ, in Him* or *in whom.*

Paul said, "Therefore, from now on, we regard no one according to the flesh..." (2 Corinthians 5:16). So get to know your true self. Become acquainted with the person you are in Him. Begin to see yourself in Christ, and become familiar with your new identity.

If you want to see yourself and know what you look like, look in the mirror. When you look in a natural mirror, you see your physical body. The only mirror you can look into and see your spirit man in Christ is the mirror of God's Word.

> *For he observes himself, goes away, and immediately forgets what kind of man he was. But he who looks into the perfect law of liberty and continues in it, and is not a forgetful hearer but a doer of the work, this one will be blessed in what he does.*
>
> —James 1:24-25

Look at yourself in the mirror of God's Word, and begin to say what God says about you. Don't let your view of yourself be based on age, race or nationality. You are a new creation in Christ. Your old man is dead. You've been raised up with Him and are filled with the very life of God. You may have had a shady past, but it came to an end with a death and a burial. You are alive today, and this is a new day. You are a new person, and you have a bright future. Be encouraged! This is the Good News.

You are a brand new being. You were made by God and for God. You were made to live in the presence of God in the city of God. It's no wonder there are times you don't feel as if you fit in here in this world. You don't belong here. You are a new creation in Christ. Old things are passed away, and all things have become new.

The book of Hebrews tells of the people of faith who went before us and "...confessed that they were strangers and pilgrims on the earth. For those who say such things declare plainly that they seek a homeland" (Hebrews 11:13-14). You were made for heaven! We, like them, "desire a better, that is, a heavenly country. Therefore

God is not ashamed to be called their God, for He has prepared a city for them" (Hebrews 11:16). We belong in that city.

I read the story of an elderly missionary couple who had spent decades on the foreign field. After many years of faithful ministry, they turned the work over to their successor and began the long journey home. Their itinerary took them through London and over the Atlantic to the city of New York. It just so happened, they were aboard the same flight as the famous rock group, The Beatles, who were coming to America for the first time. When the plane landed in New York, it looked as if the whole city had come out to welcome the Beatles. The old couple could barely make their way through the crowds that were pressing toward the plane, cheering and screaming for the famous rock band.

When they finally found a quiet place to rest, the old missionary looked at his wife sadly and said, "Honey, I'm so disappointed. The Beatles are not even from here, and they get a heroes' welcome. We've come back to our homeland after giving our lives in service to God, and there's not even one person here to welcome us home."

"No, honey! That's not true!" the wife looked back at her husband with a smile and said, "We're not home yet!"

This world is not our home, so we're not home yet. We've been born again, and we belong in the City of God. We are new creations with a new destination. When we finally do make the journey to our heavenly home, we'll get our own heroes' welcome.

CHAPTER 10

A REVELATION OF RIGHTEOUSNESS

Sin and its consequences produced thousands of years of separation from God. Guilt, condemnation and separation are words that describe fallen humanity during the years after the original sin in the garden of Eden. Isaiah 57:20-21 described man's fallen state so aptly, "But the wicked are like the troubled sea, When it cannot rest, Whose waters cast up mire and dirt. 'There is no peace,' Says my God, 'for the wicked.'" It was sad but true. There was no peace in the heart of man. There was no peace with God and no access to God. The need for righteousness was paramount.

Early 20th century minister and author E. W. Kenyon describes the effect sin and sin consciousness has on mankind in his book *Two Kinds of Righteousness:* "The sense of condemnation has given to man an inferiority complex that makes him a coward. It robs him of faith in himself, in man, in God and His Word. This sin consciousness holds him in bondage."

The veil that hung in the Old Testament temple between the people and the Holy of Holies where God's presence dwelt was an indication that the way into the presence of God was not yet made. This veil separated and blocked people from God's presence and served as a reminder that man was sinful and unfit to approach God.

In Matthew's account of the crucifixion, we find out what happened to that veil which symbolized the barrier that stood between God and man.

> *And Jesus cried out again with a loud voice, and yielded up His spirit. Then, behold, the veil of the temple was torn in two from top to bottom; and the earth quaked, and the rocks were split.*
>
> —Matthew 27:50-51

God ripped that veil of separation in two because the way was being made for mankind to return to the presence of God as He had originally intended.

The experience Israel had at Mount Sinai is another reminder of just how far sin and unrighteousness had separated man from God. God came down in a cloud on Mount Sinai to speak with Moses, and the people watched from a distance. Even this was more than they could bear. There were lightenings and thunder, and the voice of God was so awesome the people begged Moses to ask God not to speak to them directly. They would rather have God speak to Moses, and let him tell them what God said. This was not God's best, however, He honored their request. Because of their sinful condition, God was forced to relate to the people this way until righteousness could be restored.

If man was ever to approach God freely again, a radical change was necessary. For man to have the kind of fellowship and communion with the Father that would satisfy His heart, man had to be made righteous. Righteousness was an absolute must. It had to be included in the new birth.

> **"God's very own righteousness is imparted to every believer the instant he or she is born again."**

For He made Him who knew no sin to be sin for us, that we might become the righteousness of God in Him.

—2 Corinthians 5:21

When any person is born again, the new nature is imparted, and righteousness becomes a reality through Jesus Christ. This is not a righteousness that is merely acceptable by human standards; it is the righteousness of God. It is imparted to every believer the instant he or she is born again. Understanding this is vital if we are to enjoy our new standing with God through the new birth.

According to *Strong's Greek Dictionary*, the Greek word for *righteousness* is *dikaiosune,* and it is defined as *the state of him who is as he ought to be, a condition acceptable to God.* In other words, there is a condition or a way people "ought to be." This condition is called righteousness. This does not mean that those who have been made righteous are just okay or good enough. It means the being of a person or the spirit of man is as it "ought to be" according to God's standards. No one is this way until he or she receives a new nature through Jesus Christ.

Vines Dictionary of New Testament Words defines *righteousness* as *the character or quality of being right* or *right-wise-ness*. This means being right as opposed to being wrong. This is not in reference to behavior or works, but it specifically refers to the nature of a man or woman or the very condition of their being or spirit.

In order to walk with God, we had to be right and acceptable to Him. We had to measure up to His standards. God has a standard or measure of what right is, and nothing less will do. He calls this standard the righteousness of God. People cannot live up to it on their own or work their way into it. If God hadn't given it to us, we would have never been able to receive it.

Consider what the apostle Paul said to us in Romans 3.

> *For all have sinned and fall short of the glory of God, being justified freely by His grace through the redemption that is in Christ Jesus.*
>
> —Romans 3:23-24

The word *justified* is an accounting term, and it means *raised to a required standard.* So, in other words, God raised us to His required standard through the work of Christ. Therefore, we have no more condemnation, no more separation, no more guilt and no more inferiority. We are what God wants us to be; we are what He expects us to be. Not only did we need to be forgiven of our past, present and future sins, but also, our nature needed to be changed. At the new birth, we were forgiven, and we were changed.

Consider this quote from E.W. Kenyon from his book, *Two Kinds of Righteousness.*

> *No man can stand right with God simply by having his sins pardoned. It would leave the old nature that produced those sins still master of the situation. There must be a new creation.*

God made us completely new through Jesus Christ, and when He did, He made us what he wanted us to be. We could never be good enough on our own merits, so we had to have God's righteousness transferred to us.

> *Man must be restored to perfect fellowship with the Father and it must be done upon legal grounds. God becomes our righteousness.*
>
> —*Two Kinds of Righteousness*
> by E.W. Kenyon

Peter says the same thing in a different way.

> *By which have been given to us exceedingly great and precious promises, that through these you may be partakers of the divine nature, having escaped the corruption that is in the world through lust.*
>
> —2 Peter 1:4

We now have the divine nature in us, the nature or the character of God. God's nature is righteous, and our nature is now righteous. We have the same quality of righteousness in us as God has in Him, and it was given to us at the new birth.

No one has to tell God right from wrong. He is right. Therefore, He can define what right is in any situation. We read many examples in the Old Testament books of Leviticus and Deuteronomy where God told the people how to act and what to do in numerous situations. It was as if they had to have right living explained in detail. We call that "the Law." It was a series of rules given to define right behavior, and it acted as an indicator of sin. The Law was given to curb sin and ungodliness. It wasn't effective because it didn't change anyone; it just made them aware of their sinful condition.

> *For the law made nothing perfect; on the other hand, there is the bringing in of a better hope, through which we draw near to God.*
>
> —Hebrews 7:19

God had better plans for us through the better covenant, which was yet to come. He gave them some insight into the future impartation of His righteous nature in the book of Deuteronomy, and these words were quoted again in Hebrews.

> *"This is the covenant that I will make with them after those days, says the Lord: I will put My laws into their hearts, and in their minds I will write them."*
>
> —Hebrews 10:16

God's will for us was that we experience righteousness personally. He didn't want us to read about it on paper and struggle to live it in real life. He wanted us to be righteous by our very nature. He looked forward to the day when He could write His laws in our hearts and minds. That day has come, and He has downloaded His righteousness into our hearts. It happened instantly when we were saved. We became the very righteousness of God. We will never be more righteous than we are right now. We are ready to meet with God, stand in His presence and commune with Him because we are righteous in Christ.

The divine nature is righteous, holy and acceptable to God. We are not simply trying to be these things or trying to live up to a certain standard, but this is what we have become through our relationship with Jesus. This is who we are. We don't need to have "right" defined by Old Testament laws any more. This is a new day—a day of grace and liberty. We are to walk in the spirit and put on the new man.

When we live from the inside out, listen to our hearts and obey that inward witness, we instinctively know right from wrong. We know what right is the same way God knows it, by our very nature. We can live a life pleasing to God and be forever free from guilt and shame.

> *There is therefore now no condemnation to those who are in Christ Jesus, who do not walk according to the flesh, but according to the Spirit.*
>
> —Romans 8:1

The New Testament continually encourages us to live from the inside out with instructions like *walk in the spirit, put on the new man, be spiritually minded, walk in love.* The emphasis in the Old Testament was outward acts or works. The emphasis in the New Testament is the spirit man or living from the inside out. That's where the new nature abides. The new birth has made the inward man a safe guide. The believer is encouraged to develop a listening ear and to hear and obey that inward voice.

The new nature on the inside has completely changed man's relationship with sin. Look at these incredible words in 1 John:

> *Whoever has been born of God does not sin, for His seed remains in him; and he cannot sin, because he has been born of God.*
>
> —1 John 3:9

The Amplified Bible says it this way:

> *No one born (begotten) of God [deliberately, knowingly, and habitually] practices sin, for God's nature abides in him [His principle of life, the divine sperm, remains permanently within him]; and he cannot practice sinning because he is born (begotten) of God.*
>
> —1 John 3:9 (AMP)

The new nature abides within, so we live from the inside out. The new birth has made the inward man a safe guide for the born-again man or woman. Sin is not something the new creation wants to practice. That doesn't mean that a Christian will never sin again, but sin is not something the Christian wants to practice habitually. When a sinner becomes a Christian, he or she is ruined when it comes to sinful behavior. The "want to" on the inside is gone. The Christian has become the righteousness of God.

> *Therefore, if anyone is in Christ, he is a new creation; old things have passed away; behold, all things have become new.*
>
> —2 Corinthians 5:17

This new creation is righteous. In Christ, God made you everything He wanted you to be.

> *For we are His workmanship, created in Christ Jesus for good works, which God prepared beforehand that we should walk in them.*
>
> —Ephesians 2:10

The New Living Translation says, "We are God's masterpiece." He made us, and He is satisfied with His work. God has revealed an amazing confidence in His new creations. He has a divine confidence in every believer. This is shown in the new way He relates to us in the New Testament. In fact, notice the number of times we are invited to ask Him for our desires.

> *If you abide in Me, and My words abide in you, you will ask what you desire, and it shall be done for you.*
>
> —John 15:7

Until now you have asked nothing in My name. Ask, and you will receive, that your joy may be full.

—John 16:24

Therefore I say to you, whatever things you ask when you pray, believe that you receive them, and you will have them.

—Mark 11:24

The Weust Bible translation of John 15:7 says, "Ask whatever your heart desires." God trusts our hearts. After all, it is His workmanship. He wants us to know that if the thing we desire is a desire of the spirit man, He will gladly grant it. We are so much like Him that if we want it, He wants it. Our desires are His desires, and His desires are our desires. He didn't make this offer to Old Testament believers; they weren't born again. They didn't have the new nature of righteousness. Yet, today righteousness is a reality in the heart of every believer. God believes in His new creations.

E.W. Kenyon said it this way in his book *Two Kinds of Righteousness:*

> *God takes the sinner just as he is. No matter how deep in sin he has gone, the new birth will straighten him out. All the works he does are works of sin. God does not want them. God's nature drives out the sin nature and makes him a new creation. All the sins of the old creation are remitted instantaneously.*

"For we are God's masterpiece…" (Ephesians 2:10 NLT). We went from sinners to the righteousness of God. That's good news. We can begin to enjoy a new life in Christ immediately. No probation period, no waiting list. In fact, everything God has for you in Christ is yours right now.

CHAPTER 11

EFFECTS OF RIGHTEOUSNESS

Mankind is plagued with a sense of guilt and for a good reason. Without God, the heart of man is desperately wicked, and the sense of unworthiness can be crippling. Some give in to these feelings by accepting an image of inferiority. Others try to ignore them, but everyone deals with the effects of guilt and sin. Too often, people live with a sense of impending doom that comes from knowing that something is not right. Proverbs 28:1 says, "The wicked flee when no one pursues." Without a doubt, paranoia, fear, unworthiness and shame are all the results of sin consciousness.

Understanding that we have been made the righteousness of God by way of a new nature—accepted and approved by God—is life changing. All of the feelings of guilt, condemnation and inferiority flooding the human consciousness through sin are removed by the work of Christ and a revelation of righteousness.

The prophet Isaiah explained it this way.

> *The work of righteousness will be peace, and the effect of righteousness, quietness and*

assurance forever.

—Isaiah 32:17

It's difficult to fully describe the impact of this new nature in the life of a believer. Yet, this new condition of righteousness has the opposite affect than that of sin. God's purpose for redemption was to return us to the presence of God, therefore, righteousness was essential. Not only can we go into His presence, but because of what Jesus did, we belong there. We're no longer unworthy and unfit, but we're holy and accepted. We're the very righteousness of God. We are fellow citizens with the saints and members of the household of God (Ephesians 2:19).

Notice what Ephesians 1 tell us that God has done for us.

To the praise of the glory of His grace, by which He made us accepted in the Beloved.

—Ephesians 1:6

God made us "accepted." There was nothing we could do to become accepted or acceptable in our own strength or by our own performance, so He did it for us. Because of His great work of redemption, we are not rejected but accepted. We were chosen in Him before the foundation of the world (Ephesians 1:4).

And you, who once were alienated and enemies in your mind by wicked works, yet now He has reconciled in the body of His flesh through death, to present you holy, and

blameless, and above reproach in His sight.
—Colossians 1:21-22

We are more suited to stand in the presence of God today than we are to be involved in evil and sin. The fear and dread that came from knowing deep down on the inside that something wasn't right are gone when God's new nature is imparted.

> *In righteousness you shall be established; You shall be far from oppression, for you shall not fear; And from terror, for it shall not come near you.*
>
> —Isaiah 54:14

Notice that oppression, fear and terror shall not come near you. It didn't say you wouldn't have quite as much trouble with these negative forces. The scripture said they wouldn't come near you. That means, when you enter a room, oppression, fear and terror have to leave. They can't come near you because you are established in righteousness.

> "You've gone from deserving to die to having every right to live and do the will of God."

Think about it. What you had coming was the wages of sin—death, but what you received instead was the benefit of redemption—righteousness. You've gone from deserving to die to having every right to live and do the will of God. When you fully understand that you are

119

righteous, you realize that not only do you have a right to live, but also you have a right to everything that is necessary for life and godliness while you are living (2 Peter 1:3). Talk about a sense of well-being! No more do you walk around with a foreboding sense of doom. You can look forward to a reward and a new home in heaven that is out of this world. And, while you're in this world, you and I walk with God and enjoy His favor in our lives.

Righteousness brings with it a sense of confidence and assurance. This is the result of knowing that all is well between you and your Creator. His favor rests on your life in a tangible way. All this was necessary for God's dream to be fully realized. We had to be completely restored and justified to commune with Him freely. Our new nature has given us unprecedented access to God and His presence.

> *For through Him we both [Jews and Gentiles] have access by one Spirit to the Father.*
>
> —Ephesians 2:18 (brackets mine)

The greatest result of our redemption was gaining immediate access to the Father. Without the wonderful scriptures in Paul's Epistles, we wouldn't know how to act in God's presence. We wouldn't know what God required or expected from us. Should we crawl into His presence in fear and dread? Should we sneak in the back door and apologize for invading God's space? What should our attitude be as we approach the Most High God?

These next verses add a word of direction that you would never expect in connection with entering into His presence. The word is *boldness.*

> *According to the eternal purpose which He accomplished in Christ Jesus our Lord, in whom we have boldness and access with confidence through faith in Him.*
>
> —Ephesians 3:11-12

According to *Olive Tree's Enhanced Strong's Dictionary*, the Greek word for *boldness* is *parrēsia*, and its definition is *free and fearless confidence, cheerful courage, boldness, assurance.*

God did such a work in us that we can now come to Him with boldness, cheerful courage and fearless confidence. Only God could take sinful humanity and lift them so high and change them so much they could return to His presence as if sin had never been—as if they had never done anything wrong. Only God could restore humanity so thoroughly it's as if they had always been as He wanted them to be and able to enter the Holy of Holies with fearless confidence.

"The invitation has gone out for the sons and daughters of God to draw near—anytime, anywhere."

We see the word *boldness* again in Hebrews.

> *Therefore, brethren, having boldness to enter the Holiest by the blood of Jesus, ...let us draw*

> *near with a true heart in full assurance of faith....*
>
> —Hebrews 10:19, 22

The invitation has gone out for the sons and daughters of God to draw near—anytime, anywhere. When we do, we can come with boldness and assurance. We will never be denied or ignored. Our entrance is assured by Jesus Himself, and our acceptance is guaranteed. We've already been approved by Him. Boldness is mentioned again in Hebrews in connection with our entrance into His presence:

> *Let us therefore come boldly to the throne of grace, that we may obtain mercy and find grace to help in time of need.*
>
> —Hebrews 4:16

No problem is too big, and nothing is too small. He is available to respond to our call day and night, and He offers mercy and grace in abundance for any situation. The knowledge of our new nature in Christ inspires faith and confidence like nothing else on the earth. Stop reminding God of all your mistakes. Quit living in the past. Stand up, and approach the throne boldly with the assurance that is yours in Christ. God is waiting.

> *Beloved, if our heart does not condemn us, we have confidence toward God. And whatever we ask we receive from Him....*
>
> —1 John 3:21-22

When you know what Jesus did for you and you understand that you are the righteousness of God in Christ, your heart cannot condemn you any longer, and the confidence you need for effective prayer is real. This is not an attempt to usurp mind over matter. It is simply believing what God said about you in His Word. When you pray, things happen.

> *The effective, fervent prayer of a righteous man avails much.*
>
> —James 5:16

You are that righteous man or woman now. You have influence with God in Jesus' name. You can have faith in God's Word in your mouth like Jesus had faith in God's Word in His mouth.

> *For the eyes of the Lord are on the righteous, and His ears are open to their prayers....*
>
> —1 Peter 3:12

That's one encouraging prayer scripture. Let that soak in for a minute. God's eyes are on you, not to punish you or keep you in line, but to respond to your needs and desires. He is ready to enjoy your presence as you enjoy His presence. Righteousness has brought God and man back together. You are the apple of His eye.

It's the truth that sets the captives free. Those who are bound in sin need to hear the truths of righteousness and redemption. They are well acquainted with guilt and condemnation, but to only focus attention on what the old man has done is counterproductive. Preaching sin instead of righteousness keeps people under condemnation rather than leading them into liberty.

Christians need to hear what God has done for them and who they are in Christ in order to reprogram their minds and live the new life that God has for them. Their self-image must be renewed by God's Word. They must see themselves in the light of redemption—no longer guilty, lost and unworthy, but saved, righteous and holy.

It takes time to renew the mind, but it is absolutely essential. The only place to find your new identity is in the Word of God. No one else can see you as the person you really are in Christ. Don't look for affirmation from other sources. All the positive affirmation you'll ever need is in God's Word. Spend some time everyday looking at yourself in the mirror of God's Word. You'll be amazed at what you see.

We used several scriptures in this chapter to describe your new identity. Let's review some of the key words as they relate to you and your new life in Christ. Begin the renewal process right now. Let me encourage you to read these statements aloud:

"Because I am the righteousness of God in Christ Jesus, I have peace, quietness and assurance. I am chosen by God and accepted in the beloved. I have been reconciled, and I am holy, blameless and above reproach in His sight. I am established in righteousness. I shall not fear. I am far from oppression, and terror shall not come near me. I have access to the Father, and I approach Him with boldness and confidence in full assurance of faith. I have a limitless supply of mercy and grace to help in time of need. My heart does not condemn me, and my prayers avail much."

This simple confession was taken from scriptures used in this chapter, but the New Testament is filled with such promises that are capable of changing the way you think and giving you a brand new image of yourself.

CHAPTER 12

THE GIFT OF RIGHTEOUSNESS

In previous chapters, we've highlighted the importance of righteousness as it relates to the new creation. We've also looked at the tremendous, radical impact righteousness has on the life of the believer. But there is yet another aspect of righteousness that cannot be overlooked. The fact that righteousness is a gift must be fully understood in order for believers to truly appreciate how it's positioned them in Christ and opened the door to grace and faith.

To understand the gift of righteousness, first and foremost, we must understand that it's not earned but given freely.

> *...those who receive abundance of grace and of the gift of righteousness will reign in life through the One, Jesus Christ.*
>
> —Romans 5:17

There was a price to pay for righteousness to be restored to mankind, so in that sense it wasn't free. But, thank God, Jesus paid that price for us. If God had waited for man to earn right-standing, it never would have happened. Rather than giving us what we deserved, God freely gave us all the good He intended for us. This was the only way we could become what God wanted us to be.

God introduced a whole new system in the New Testament. It is the concept of grace and faith. This process is foreign to the natural mind, but it was the only way God could fully restore man to fellowship with Himself and fulfill His vision for man. Natural man struggles with the idea that the priceless treasures offered in the New Testament are given freely. God's most valuable gifts—forgiveness, the new birth, righteousness and adoption into His family—are given to people who are undeserving.

> *And you, who once were alienated and enemies in your mind by wicked works, yet now He has reconciled in the body of His flesh through death, to present you holy, and blameless, and above reproach in His sight.*
>
> —Colossians 1:21-22

If we are going to be partakers of His grace, we must get used to the fact that we will always be indebted to God and His son Jesus Christ. We were "alienated and enemies" with no standing with God whatsoever. We had nothing to offer Him for our redemption. Yet, He gave freely and generously.

There's no way we can repay Jesus for what He has given us. This is the way the New Covenant works. God had so much to give, it would have been impossible to do it any other way. Grace makes everything God has available to every person—no limits, no favoritism, no politics. The only limiting factor is faith. Every person on earth gets as much of God's grace as he or she chooses to believe and receive.

> *For by grace you have been saved through faith, and that not of yourselves; it is the gift of God, not of works, lest anyone should boast.*
>
> —Ephesians 2:8-9

Man has a natural leaning toward religion or what Paul calls "works." Yet, as you can see in Ephesians 2:9, salvation is "not of works lest anyone should boast." Natural man wants to boast or add his works to God's grace. People are proud of their accomplishments and mistakenly think they deserve God's blessings because of what they've done. "*I go to church every time the door is open.*" "*I give my money to God every time they pass the plate.*" "*I pray every day.*" "*I read my Bible every day.*" They make these statements as if these words give them some kind of inside track with God. Religion or "works" give people a way to compare themselves with others. When used in this way, it is simply a merit system based on performance that leads to pride. Their whole identity is dependent on their actions.

This is what the Bible calls, "frustrating the grace of God" in Galatians 2:21 (KJV). Nothing that God offers through redemption is available because of what a person has done. God doesn't take pity on someone or show favoritism because one person is a "better" Christian or a harder worker than another. God's redemptive blessings come freely. They come regardless of works. They come as gifts that cannot be earned. This is why Jesus told His disciples to be like children.

> *Assuredly, I say to you, whoever does not receive the kingdom of God as a little child will by no means enter it.*
>
> —Mark 10:15

Children know how to receive a free gift. They don't overthink the process. If you want to give it to them, they're ready to receive it. They don't even consider whether they deserve it or not.

The apostle Paul was dealing with religious people who wanted to turn Christianity into a religion of works. He spent a great deal of time teaching the church to receive by faith. He used Abraham as an example of someone who believed God and put no confidence in the works of the flesh.

> *For if Abraham was justified by works, he has something to boast about, but not before God. For what does the Scripture say? "Abraham believed God, and it was accounted to him for righteousness." Now to him who works, the wages are not counted as grace but as debt.*
>
> —Romans 4:2-4

Notice the phrase "...to him who works the wages are counted as debt." This is an important point. If you work for something, what you receive is determined by what you earn. Yet, when it comes to redemption, you don't want what you can earn, and you certainly don't want what you deserve. You have to leave the thinking of earnings and wages behind or you'll never get what God has for you. Come on over to the New Testament system of grace, and receive all that He has to give.

> *But to him who does not work but believes on Him who justifies the ungodly, his faith is accounted for righteousness.*
>
> —Romans 4:5

Hard work doesn't receive righteousness. It is faith in God's Word that receives the gift of righteousness. This means anybody is a candidate, because anybody can believe God's Word.

> *Therefore it is of faith that it might be according to grace, so that the promise might be sure to all the seed, not only to those who are of the law, but also to those who are of the faith of Abraham, who is the father of us all.*
>
> —Romans 4:16

Through faith the promise of righteousness is available to all. No one can work hard enough to receive it, but anyone can believe for it. On the other hand, no one is disqualified by past mistakes. You have probably heard people inquiring about salvation say, "Well, you don't know what all I've done." They believe their actions have disqualified them from receiving God's gift of righteousness, but it's not about what they've done or haven't done. Their works don't count. They have the idea that bad works have disqualified them, and good works, if they had any, would somehow qualify them. That's an example of how "works" doesn't work.

Most people think they are too bad to receive salvation, and some think they are good enough because of what they've done, so they don't need salvation. The promise (righteousness) is sure to all seed (people) through faith in Jesus (Romans 4:13). God's promise of righteousness is for "good people" and "bad people" and everyone in between. But it has nothing to do with what they've done (their works) and everything to do with what they believe.

> *For if there had been a law given which could have given life, truly righteousness would have been by the law.*
>
> —Galatians 3:21

Paul is once again making the point that the law or works is not the way to righteousness. If it had been possible to earn eternal life, God would not have sent Jesus. He would have let people earn their way to heaven, and the works program would have been the way to salvation. The truth is, no matter how good someone behaves, he or she is still a sinner. Outward actions don't change the condition of the heart.

> *But the Scripture has confined all under sin, that the promise by faith in Jesus Christ*

might be given to those who believe.

—Galatians 3:22

Faith in the promises of God is God's chosen way of salvation for the lost.

Relying on works was a big problem when the New Testament was written, and it remains a big problem today. Paul deals with it again in Romans 9 and 10. In these verses, Israel represents people who are trying to work their way to right-standing with God, and the phrase *works of the law* simply means *religious works*.

> *But Israel, pursuing the law of righteousness, has not attained to the law of righteousness. Why? Because they did not seek it by faith, but as it were, by the works of the law.*
>
> —Romans 9:31-32

Many people are following that same pattern today. They are counting on the works of the law or good behavior to make them right, but notice what Paul goes on to say in Romans 10.

> *For they being ignorant of God's righteousness, and seeking to establish their own righteousness, have not submitted to the righteousness of God. For Christ is the end of the law for righteousness to everyone who believes.*
>
> —Romans 10:3-4

133

GOOD NEWS

No one on the earth can establish his or her own righteousness. It's impossible. We don't have what it takes to make ourselves right with God. Christ is the end of the law for righteousness. No more working for something that can't be earned. We have received the gift of righteousness, and for it to really work in our lives, we must understand that it is a gift. You didn't earn it. You cannot pay for it, but you have it nonetheless.

> "You have the same righteous nature now that you will have when you get to heaven. Grace made it available, and faith has made it yours."

Righteousness is a gift, not a fruit. It doesn't grow or develop. Your understanding of righteous may grow and your knowledge of it may increase, but you will never be more righteous than you are right now. *In Christ*, you are righteous. You are ready to stand in God's presence without a hint of guilt or shame. You have the same righteous nature now that you will have when you get to heaven. Grace made it available, and faith has made it yours.

Paul goes on to explain exactly how to release your faith in God's grace for salvation.

> *That if you confess with your mouth the Lord Jesus and believe in your heart that God has raised Him from the dead, you will be saved. For with the heart one believes unto*

righteousness, and with the mouth confession is made unto salvation.

—Romans 10:9-10

This is the most simple, most powerful explanation anywhere in God's Word on how to receive the free gift of righteousness. Everyone is a candidate. Anyone can follow the instructions in Romans 10:9-10 and be saved. It's not beyond anyone's ability or over anyone's head. Rich and poor, young and old, every race and nationality can receive salvation by following the simple steps in these two verses.

Nothing less would have been acceptable to God who desires all men to be saved. He would have never made an offer that only certain people were capable of accepting or that was beyond anyone's ability to receive. The gospel message works everywhere, for everyone, all the time. As the great evangelist T. L. Osborn said, "Whosoever means, anybody can, but everybody won't."

Paul visits this same subject again in his letter to Titus:

> *But when the kindness and the love of God our Savior toward man appeared, not by works of righteousness which we have done, but according to His mercy He saved us, through the washing of regeneration and renewing of the Holy Spirit.*
>
> —Titus 3:4-5

Kenyon said, again from his book *Two Kinds of Righteousness*, "We look with fear upon any message that brings relief unless it is a message of works. We want to pray, sacrifice, confess...." Yet, righteousness is a gift. Gifts are not to be worked for because they cannot be earned. However, this does not mean we never work. We are not in any way promoting a lifestyle of laziness and inactivity. According to the Bible, we are supposed to work. We don't work to earn the gifts of God, but rather we work because we have received them.

Notice the scriptural progression in Ephesians:

> *For by grace you have been saved through faith, and that not of yourselves; it is the gift of God, not of works, lest anyone should boast. For we are His workmanship, created in Christ Jesus for good works, which God prepared beforehand that we should walk in them.*
>
> —Ephesians 2:8-10

First there is grace which provides the gifts of God. Then comes the faith to receive, and it's followed by the ability to do good works. We are His workmanship "created in Christ Jesus for good works." His grace, received by our faith, leads to good works. We aren't working to become good; we work because we are good. Good works don't produce righteousness; righteousness produces good works.

> *This is a faithful saying, and these things I want you to affirm constantly, that those who have believed in God should be careful*

to maintain good works. These things are
good and profitable to men.

—Titus 3:8

Once a person receives eternal life by faith and becomes the righteousness of God in Christ, he or she is ready to get to work. Good works are simply the result of the goodness of God on the inside, working its way to the outside. We don't work to earn God's favor or any additional blessings freely given in Christ, but the fruit of the Spirit should certainly manifest in our lives in the form of good works. We are qualified to do great things for God and for people because of the changes that have happened on the inside of us.

The apostle Paul was a hard worker, and as a result of his labors, the New Testament church flourished in the ancient world.

But by the grace of God I am what I am, and
His grace toward me was not in vain; but I
labored more abundantly than they all, yet
not I, but the grace of God which was with
me.

—1 Corinthians 15:10

Because of the power of Christ in us, we are blessed and ready to do great things for God.

CHAPTER 13

TRUTHS OF DIVINE HEALING

Physical healing was paid for by the Lord Jesus and is as much a part of our redemption as forgiveness, righteousness and the new birth. Jesus healed the sick in His own ministry and included divine healing in the Great Commission of Mark 16, where He gave the mandate to preach the gospel to every creature. The command to preach the gospel was followed by the command to lay hands on the sick with the promise that they would recover. No wonder divine healing has been called the gospel "dinner bell" and has drawn millions of people to the Lord over the past 2,000 years of the church.

The Bible has much to say on the subject of divine healing, and no book on the Good News would be complete without it. Scriptures throughout the Old Testament and the New Testament teach us on this important topic. So much, in fact, it can be a bit overwhelming when trying to study or teach or meditate on this vital topic.

As I have studied the subject of divine healing over many years, it seems to me that all the Bible's healing scriptures and healing examples naturally fall into four main categories. These headings form what I call four main pillars or foundational truths concerning divine healing.

It's helped me tremendously in understanding, studying and teaching this subject to list every scripture and each healing miracle in the ministry of Jesus under one or more of these main headings, which work together and independently. Of course, there are many other truths and statements the Bible makes regarding healing, but these four are essential when it comes to receiving healing yourself or sharing the truth of healing with others.

Four Pillars of Truth

Every healing scripture in the Bible affirms or confirms one or more of these truths. They are progressive revelation. They answer the who, what, when, why and how of divine healing and are vitally important to anyone who wants to take the journey from sickness to health. In fact, if you need some help in managing your own personal healing portfolio, I challenge you to list the healing truths you find in your Bible under one or more of these main headings for the purpose of study and meditation.

1. Sickness Is the Result of Sin and Satan.

It will be very difficult to get rid of sickness and disease if you are not sure where it came from. If there is any hint of concern that it came from God, faith is hindered until this doubt is removed. Yet, God's Word is explicit on the origin of sickness.

> *The thief does not come except to steal, and to kill, and to destroy. I have come that they may have life, and that they may have it more abundantly.*
>
> —John 10:10

Jesus came to give us abundant life. But there's no question that sickness steals, kills and destroys, and there's no question that the thief—or the devil—is responsible. There was no sickness and disease on the earth before Adam sinned. There is none in heaven, and there will be none on the earth after Satan is cast into the lake of fire.

We see very clearly in the book of Deuteronomy that sickness and disease is part of the curse of the Law, which is the result of the entrance of sin (Deuteronomy 28:21-61). After a pretty exhaustive list of sicknesses, the Bible says, "Also every sickness and every plague, which is not written in this Book of the Law..." (Deuteronomy 28:61). Thank God, "Christ has redeemed us from the curse of the law..." (Galatians 3:13).

We also see clearly throughout the Bible that in many cases sickness and demons go hand in hand.

> *How God anointed Jesus of Nazareth with the Holy Spirit and with power, who went*

about doing good and healing all who were oppressed by the devil, for God was with Him.

—Acts 10:38

"When healing comes in, sickness and disease—and everything associated with it—must go."

In Luke 13, we read where Jesus healed a woman who was bowed over and couldn't lift herself up. After her miracle Jesus said, "...Ought not this woman, being a daughter of Abraham, whom Satan hath bound, lo, these eighteen years, be loosed from this bond on the sabbath day?" (verse 16 KJV).

Evil spirits are mentioned in connection with sickness once again in the book of Acts.

Now God worked unusual miracles by the hands of Paul, so that even handkerchiefs or aprons were brought from his body to the sick, and the diseases left them and the evil spirits went out of them.

—Acts 19:11-12

Notice what happened when Philip preached to the Samaritans.

For unclean spirits, crying with a loud voice, came out of many who were possessed; and many who were paralyzed and lame were healed.

—Acts 8:7

In these cases the sicknesses, infirmities and devils all left at the same time. When healing comes in, sickness and disease—and everything associated with it—must go. Jesus paid the price for our healing.

2. Divine Healing Is the Will of God.

Almost every healing scripture could be included in this category. However, there are a few instances that specifically show that divine healing is the will of God. For one thing, Jesus never turned away anyone with sickness by telling them it wasn't God's will to heal them. There is not one case in which Jesus used sickness and disease to teach someone. If using sickness to teach someone a lesson is as common as some people teach today, you would think we would have had at least one example of it in the New Testament.

Not knowing for sure that it's God's will to heal, undermines faith and makes it almost impossible to receive divine healing. So let's focus on a few scriptures that establish that healing is God's will for every person.

Now a leper came to Him, [Jesus] imploring Him, kneeling down to Him and saying to Him, "If You are willing, You can make me clean."

—Mark 1:40 (brackets mine)

The leper didn't know the will of God, but he soon found out. In fact, Jesus made His will clear to the leper—and every one of us. "Then Jesus, moved with compassion, stretched out His hand and touched him, and said to him, 'I am willing; be cleansed'" (Mark 1:41).

Jesus is still willing today.

In many instances, Jesus healed whole crowds of people. He healed *them all.*

> And the whole multitude sought to touch Him, for power went out from Him and healed them all.
>
> —Luke 6:19

If healing was not God's will for everyone, why did Jesus heal them all? He didn't separate them into two groups. He didn't put the people God was willing to heal in one group and the people God was not willing to heal in another. No. He healed them all. Matthew 12:15, Matthew 14:14 and Matthew 14:34-36 also speak of Jesus healing *them all.*

These examples provide further proof that healing is God's will for everyone. He healed them all because it was God's will to heal *them all.*

> ...And as many as touched Him were made well.
>
> —Mark 6:56

> Is anyone among you sick? Let him call for the elders of the church, and let them pray over

him, anointing him with oil in the name of the Lord. And the prayer of faith will save the sick, and the Lord will raise him up....

—James 5:14-15

Notice James didn't say, "If it's God's will, He will raise them up." He said, "Is anyone among you sick?" It is implied here that healing is the will of God for any sick person. He didn't say this would work for some sick people or certain sick people. He made the offer to any sick person.

3. Divine Healing Is Part of Our Redemption.

Look with me at a foundational healing scripture that establishes how forgiveness *and* healing are part of redemption.

But He was wounded for our transgressions, He was bruised for our iniquities; the chastisement for our peace was upon Him, and by His stripes we are healed.

—Isaiah 53:5

Every Christian believes that Jesus suffered in order that forgiveness could be offered to the whole world. The gospel clearly reveals that Jesus paid the penalty for sins. But there's so much more. Isaiah 53:5 not only says the price for sins was paid, but it also says that the price for healing was paid. If we can believe that Jesus suffered in order to purchase forgiveness, why can't we also believe

His suffering—the stripes He endured—purchased our healing? The Bible often puts healing and forgiveness together. Healing and forgiveness were purchased at the same time in the same work of redemption.

> *Bless the Lord, O my soul, and forget not all His benefits: who forgives all your iniquities, who heals all your diseases.*
>
> —Psalm 103:2-3

> *Who Himself bore our sins in His own body on the tree, that we, having died to sins, might live for righteousness—by whose stripes you were healed.*
>
> —1 Peter 2:24

Notice how, in the previous two verses, healing and forgiveness were mentioned together. That's because *healing is part of our redemption.* It was never supposed to be separated from forgiveness. The two were purchased together, and they are supposed to be offered together. The Great Commission begins with "preach the gospel to every creature" and ends with "lay hands on the sick and they shall recover" (Mark 16:15-18).

Another example of forgiveness and healing working hand in hand can be found in Luke 5 where the paralytic was let down through the roof as Jesus taught the people. Not only do we see someone receiving healing by faith, but we also see Jesus combined healing and forgiveness together to the astonishment of the crowd.

Which is easier, to say, 'Your sins are forgiven you,' or to say, 'Rise up and walk'? But that you may know that the Son of Man has power on earth to forgive sins"—He said to the man who was paralyzed, "I say to you, arise, take up your bed, and go to your house."

—Luke 5:23-24

Jesus offers both healing and forgiveness because they are both included in His redemptive work. That was true then, and it's true now. Jesus Christ is the same yesterday, today and forever (Hebrews 13:8).

4. Divine Healing Is Received by Faith.

Volumes have been written on the subject of faith and rightfully so. The majority of people who came to Jesus for healing received it by faith, and it is still the same today. Faith is something we do; God won't do it for us. Those who practiced the principles of faith when coming to Jesus for healing received their answer every time. The instances where people came to Jesus and received their miracles by faith also serve as examples to us. If we learn to do as they did, we can get what they got.

When the woman with the issue of blood was healed, Jesus let the whole world know how she received her miracle:

And He said to her, "Daughter, your faith has made you well. Go in peace, and be healed of your affliction."

—Mark 5:34

If her faith could make her whole, your faith can make you whole.

Notice Jesus' words to Jairus after it was known that his daughter was dead.

> *As soon as Jesus heard the word that was spoken, He said to the ruler of the synagogue, "Do not be afraid; only believe."*
>
> —Mark 5:36

Notice what Jesus told the father who had a son with a deaf and dumb spirit.

> *Jesus said to him, "If you can believe, all things are possible to him who believes."*
>
> —Mark 9:23

Notice what Jesus said to the two blind men who came for healing.

> *And when He had come into the house, the blind men came to Him. And Jesus said to them, "Do you believe that I am able to do this?" They said to Him, "Yes, Lord." Then He touched their eyes, saying, "According to your faith let it be to you."*
>
> —Matthew 9:28-29

There are other methods Jesus sometimes used to deliver healing to people, such as gifts of the Spirit—gifts of healings, working of miracles and others. However, receiving healing by faith worked each time and every time. Those who received by faith didn't wait for Jesus to touch them; they touched Jesus. They didn't wait for an invitation or a visitation. They chose the time and the place where they met Jesus, and they received their healing.

Included in this chapter is only a partial list of those who received their healing by faith through the ministry of Jesus as recorded in the Gospels. What is important to note is that faith works the same today as it did back then. People are still being healed by faith today, and so can you. God is no respecter of persons. These examples and others in the Gospels serve as encouragement for us to stop doubting, and start believing for the blessings of God.

We could add many more scriptures and healing examples from the ministry of Jesus to each of the four categories above. In fact, there is so much information on the subject of divine healing that volumes have been written on it. Our goal in this chapter was to lay a good foundation, so you can begin a lifelong study of divine healing and health because, without a doubt, healing is part of our redemption. And it's available to everyone, which is definitely Good News.

CHAPTER 14

NO BETTER NEWS

The Good News of the gospel not only offers forgiveness and divine healing, but it also contains the power to change the world around us. The gospel is not an insignificant message for emotionally weak people looking to escape reality. It's not a crutch as some have said. The Good News of the gospel is more powerful than the constant drumbeat of bad news coming from media outlets the world over, every day. In fact, what Jesus did for us will eventually impact every part of God's creation. No matter what it may look like, God is greater than evil, and grace is greater than sin.

> ""The Good News of the gospel is more powerful than the constant drumbeat of bad news coming from media outlets the world over every day."

The apostle Paul said it this way:

> ...*where sin abounded, grace abounded much more.*
>
> —Romans 5:20

This scripture is well known and often quoted. We know the Bible is true, but it appears that sin is outdoing grace in the world all the time. It seems that sin continues to abound, and at times, sin and the bad news resulting from it can be overwhelming. How is it possible for grace to be abounding much more than sin?

The Message version of the Bible says, "When it's sin versus grace, grace wins hands down" (Romans 5:20). Is this true or is this what we tell people just to make them feel better? Let's take a look at the truth.

What God did for mankind through Jesus far exceeds what Satan did to mankind through Adam. In Romans 5, Paul makes this point over and over again. He explains that what God did for us is much more powerful than anything the devil did to us. Jesus, the second Adam, was able to undo what Satan had done to man through the fall.

> ...*For if by the one man's offense many died, much more the grace of God and the gift by the grace of the one Man, Jesus Christ, abounded to many.*
>
> —Romans 5:15

What Jesus did for us is much greater in the positive than what sin did to us in the negative. In Romans 5, Paul uses the words *much more* to make this point.

Notice these words again in verse 17.

> *For if by the one man's offense death reigned through the one, much more those who receive abundance of grace and of the gift of righteousness will reign in life through the One, Jesus Christ.*
>
> —Romans 5:17

Adam brought death, but Jesus brought life to those who receive the abundance of grace. Life is greater than death, and grace is greater than sin, just as God is greater than the devil and light is more powerful than darkness. What God did for us is "much more" than what Satan could do against us.

The grace of God released through Jesus was powerful enough to turn sinners into saints.

> *For as by one man's disobedience many were made sinners, so also by one Man's obedience many will be made righteous.*
>
> —Romans 5:19

The truth is, grace has already won. Jesus has already defeated the enemy, and greater is He that is in you than he that is in the world (1 John 4:4).

Things may not appear that way, and this is why. Sin has been going full speed ahead for more than 6,000 years. It is in full manifestation—all around us, every day. But the church—until now—has only received a down payment of the grace of God. The full payment is yet to come.

> *Now He who establishes us with you in Christ and has anointed us is God, who also has sealed us and given us the Spirit in our hearts as a guarantee.*
>
> —2 Corinthians 1:21-22

That word *guarantee* in verse 22, in *Strong's Greek Dictionary* means *down payment.* With that in mind, read another verse a few chapters over.

> *Now He who has prepared us for this very thing is God, who also has given us the Spirit as a guarantee [down payment].*
>
> —2 Corinthians 5:5 (brackets mine)

According to the Word, we have only received the down payment of our inheritance.

> *In Him you also trusted, after you heard the word of truth, the gospel of your salvation; in whom also, having believed, you were sealed with the Holy Spirit of promise, who is the guarantee of our inheritance until the redemption of the purchased possession, to the praise of His glory.*
>
> —Ephesians 1:13-14

Usually a down payment is smaller than the rest of the payment, just a small percentage of the full payment. We have received the down payment until the *redemption of the purchased possession*. It's already purchased! The price has been paid in full, complete redemption of all of creation from the damages done by sin. The down payment has been made, but there is more to come—much more.

> "The truth is that the Good News is the best news on the planet."

Most of what we teach and preach in our churches today is concerning the down payment, and the down payment is so good; it's almost hard to believe. The gifts of the Spirit, our deliverance from the kingdom of darkness, the infilling of the Holy Spirit, divine healing and God's supernatural provision are all part of the down payment. In fact, the most powerful result of the down payment has occurred in our spirits through the new birth.

The world around us can't see the dramatic changes that have taken place in our lives due to the new birth and the gifts of God in us. They may be tempted to think that God isn't doing anything in the world today. They may be tempted to think there is no God or if there is a God, He's detached and uninterested in our lives. But that's not true. God is working on the inside of us. What He's done in His children is revolutionary, life changing and eternal. Yet, what's happened so far is nothing compared to what He's going to do.

> *But we speak the wisdom of God in a mystery, the hidden wisdom which God*

> *ordained before the ages for our glory, which*
> *none of the rulers of this age knew; for had*
> *they known, they would not have crucified*
> *the Lord of glory. But as it is written: "Eye*
> *has not seen, nor ear heard, Nor have entered*
> *into the heart of man The things which God*
> *has prepared for those who love Him."*
>
> —1 Corinthians 2:7-9

The truth is that the Good News is the best news on the planet. God, through His grace, has so thoroughly defeated sin and Satan that one day, there won't be any evidence that they even existed.

The Good News is so good the bad news doesn't matter.

If you are a Christian, the bad news won't last forever, but the Good News will. You've heard this before, and it is true: The best is yet to come! What is yet to come is so much better. The half has never yet been told.

One of the great things yet to come is the redemption of our bodies. We are going to get new bodies. Grace has already paid for them, and they are part of the full payment that is imminent.

> *For we know that the whole creation groans*
> *and labors with birth pangs together until*
> *now. Not only that, but we also who have*
> *the firstfruits of the Spirit, even we ourselves*
> *groan within ourselves, eagerly waiting for*
> *the adoption, the redemption of our body.*
>
> —Romans 8:22-23

I was speaking at a church in Texas years ago, and we were having a church-wide dinner following the Sunday service. An older gentleman sat down across from me and informed me that he had a question to ask. Evidently he had been thinking ahead, way ahead, and he began to talk about death and heaven.

"I am a Christian," he said. "I believe I'm a spirit, and I live in a body."

"Yes," I said. "That's what I believe and teach as well."

"So when I die," he continued, "They will put my body in the grave, and my spirit will go to heaven."

"Yes," I said, quoting 2 Corinthians 5:8, which says when we are absent from the body, we are present with the Lord. I added, "If you're a Christian, when you die, your spirit will go to heaven."

"Good! That's where I want to be," he said.

"Praise God!" I said, glad all his questions were answered.

Then he hit me with the big one. "Well," he said, "if I'm a spirit in heaven with Jesus, that's all I want. I'm happy with that. Why do I have to come back to the earth and get my body at the resurrection? Why? If I'm already in heaven with Jesus, I don't care if I get my body back. I'm not sure I want to get my body back. Why do I have to get my body back? Why?"

At the time, I was barely 30 years old, traveling around the country in a motor home, preaching in churches with a wife and two small kids. The last thing I was thinking about was the resurrection of the dead. I had no idea how to answer his question and hadn't spent a minute even thinking about it.

So I was about to say, "I don't know." But out of my mouth came these words, "It's the principle of the thing!" No sooner had I said that than the answer came by revelation.

I said, "You may not want your body back, but this isn't about you. You were never supposed to lose your body. It was not made to die, but sin came and made it mortal. Death doomed mankind.

"Praise God, when Jesus came to redeem us from sin, He came to undo everything that sin had done to us. He came to get back everything sin had stolen from us, including your body. So a 50 percent or a 60 percent redemption might be ok with you, but this is not about you. It's about Him. It's about Jesus.

"Jesus came to get everything back, and that's exactly what He did. He got it all back, including your body. He paid the price so you could have a new one just like His. So, you're going to get a new body, and you're going to like it!"

With his eyes open wide, the older gentleman stared at me and nodded. He began to understand—and I did, too—just how much Jesus has done for us all.

At the resurrection, we who are alive in Christ and remain will be changed. Those who are already asleep (dead) in Christ will be raised, but we will all get brand new bodies.

> *Behold, I tell you a mystery: We shall not all sleep, but we shall all be changed—in a moment, in the twinkling of an eye, at the last trumpet. For the trumpet will sound, and the dead will be raised incorruptible, and we shall be changed. For this corruptible must put on incorruption, and this mortal must put on immortality. So when this corruptible has put on incorruption, and this mortal has put on immortality, then shall be brought to pass the saying that is written: "Death is swallowed up in victory. O Death, where is your sting? O Hades, where is your victory?"*
>
> —1 Corinthians 15:51-55

There will be no more sickness, disease or death in our new bodies. Our new bodies won't get tired or age or grow old.

> *For we who are in this tent groan, being burdened, not because we want to be unclothed, but further clothed, that mortality may be swallowed up by life. Now He who has prepared us for this very thing is God, who also has given us the Spirit as a guarantee.*
>
> —2 Corinthians 5:4-5

Paul says we continue to *groan* until we get our new bodies. In the original Greek language, the word *groan* means *we all groan together until our bodies are released from the effects of mortality.* The tent that is mentioned is the physical body. It will be swallowed up by life. The eternal life that is in our spirits now will extend its domain to our physical bodies.

> *For our citizenship is in heaven, from which we also eagerly wait for the Savior, the Lord Jesus Christ, who will transform our lowly body that it may be conformed to His glorious body....*
>
> —Philippians 3:20-21

Our new bodies will be just like His body—glorious, ever young, vibrant and full of God's power. When Jesus appeared to the disciples in Luke 24:39, He said, "Behold My hands and My feet, that it is I Myself: handle Me and see, for a spirit does not have flesh and bones as you see Me have." Jesus was proud of His new body, and you will be proud of yours, too. It will run on the very life of God. It will be forever young, the way it was supposed to be before sin came into the world.

Our bodies are not the only thing that will change as the full payment of grace comes into manifestation. Paul said the whole creation groans and labors together with birth pangs unto that day. The whole universe is going to change.

> *But the day of the Lord will come as a thief in the night, in which the heavens [universe] will pass away with a great noise, and the elements will melt with fervent heat; both the earth and the works that are in it will be burned up.*
>
> —2 Peter 3:10 (brackets mine)

This entire creation is going to be burned up and literally born again. Your spirit has been born again. Your body will be born again, and eventually the whole universe will be born again. It will be a very similar process to what you have already experienced in your spirit. Old things will pass away and all things will become new.

> *Looking for and hastening the coming of the day of God, because of which the heavens [the universe] will be dissolved, being on fire, and the elements will melt with fervent heat? Nevertheless we, according to His promise, look for new heavens and a new earth in which righteousness dwells.*
>
> —2 Peter 3:12-13 (brackets mine)

God is going to make a new universe and a new earth. This one was polluted by sin and ruined, and it cannot be recycled. It must pass away and be born again and replaced with a new earth and a new universe.

In Revelation, John picks up where Peter left off in 2 Peter.

> *Now I saw a new heaven and a new earth, for the first heaven and the first earth had passed away. Also there was no more sea.*
>
> —Revelation 21:1

God will make all things new. John goes on to tell us that heaven—the city of God—will come down to the new earth, and God will dwell with mankind. He will be our God, and we will be His people. Together we will live forever in this new, sinless paradise.

And it gets better.

> *And God will wipe away every tear from their eyes; there shall be no more death, nor sorrow, nor crying. There shall be no more pain, for the former things have passed away."*
>
> —Revelation 21:4

God will wipe away every tear from our eyes. He will remove every bit of residue that sin has left on our being. Any scars or wounds that we may have, any regrets or mistakes or failures that cause us pain will be permanently removed by God Himself. Jesus has already paid for it, and the full manifestation is coming.

This is the Good News, and it is coming soon. There is coming a day when new creations—you and I—will live in a new universe with new bodies, and God will dwell in our midst. The devil and evil will be thrown into the Lake of Fire, and nothing will be left that sin infected.

Grace has so completely defeated sin that there is coming a day in which it will be as if sin never existed, as if there never was a devil. It will be as if there never was a fall in the garden of Eden. It will be as if you never sinned or never made a mistake. It's all because of Jesus. It's about what He did—not about what you did. "… Where sin abounded, grace has abounded much more" (Romans 5:20).

Then Jesus will step forward and speak these words:

> *And He said to me, "It is done! I am the Alpha and the Omega, the Beginning and the End....*
>
> —Revelation 21:6

It's not over until Jesus says it's over. And it's not over yet. When He's finished, you won't recognize this place. It will be exactly what He intended from the beginning—a new heaven and a new earth in which righteousness dwells.

We are in the middle of the fulfillment of a dream that God has had from before the foundation of the world, and it will be accomplished. Nothing can stop God from doing what He sets out to do. Not sin. Not the devil. Not kings. Not rulers of the earth. Nothing and no one can stop God's plan from coming to pass. He is going to have the family He so desired.

> *That in the ages to come He might show the exceeding riches of His grace in His kindness toward us in Christ Jesus.*
>
> —Ephesians 2:7

We will be on display forever as examples of what God does for those He loves. It may take all of eternity for Him to share with us the riches of His grace. This is God's dream, and we are the beneficiaries. I wouldn't want to miss it for anything in the world.

GOOD NEWS

This is no fairy tale with a happy ending or wishful thinking for those who are trying to escape reality. These things are true, and they will come to pass for the family of God, in due time.

This is the Good News that we preach. Where sin abounded, grace abounded much more is absolutely true. And there's no better news.

The Good News is so good the bad news doesn't matter.

CHAPTER 15

OUR MESSAGE

The gospel message or the Good News is the greatest message in the world. It has no competition. It is the only message that gives the world real answers to life's greatest questions. We should never be intimidated into thinking that the Good News is antiquated or irrelevant. Not only does the gospel have a place in the modern world, but it's also exactly what the world needs to hear. It is God's answer to the world's greatest problem, which is sin.

God chose to give the world an answer—a Savior—and His name is Jesus. It is God's will that this wonderful news be shared with the world through believers. We should never feel as if this message isn't adequate or somehow has been left behind by modern life. It is not something to ignore; it's something to celebrate. Even in Paul's day, the message was controversial, and he felt the need to make his position known.

> *For I am not ashamed of the gospel of Christ....*
>
> —Romans 1:16

There has been a stigma attached to the gospel message from the beginning. Paul said it was a stumbling block to the Jews and foolishness to the Greeks (1 Corinthians 1:23). It will never be popular to the worldly minded, but it's the answer that is needed, whether it is approved of or not.

It answers the most important questions and gives insight into the meaning of life like no other explanation on the earth. It begins with the creation of the heavens and the earth and ends with the Father God living in the midst of His family in the new heavens and the new earth. The events in between make up the greatest story ever told.

It's a mystery and an adventure, a romance and a tragedy. It's a love story about a God who would not give up on His dream, no matter the cost. It's filled with special effects and twists and turns that are unexpected and surprising. It includes heroes and villains, and it has an ending that goes beyond the imagination. "...Eye has not seen, nor ear heard...the things which God has prepared for those who love Him" (1 Corinthians 2:9).

These gospel truths serve as an anchor for the soul. They give a sense of direction and purpose in a world filled with challenges and uncertainty. The great mysteries of man's origin and destiny are masterfully answered in the pages of God's Word as He reveals where we came from, who we are, why we're here and where we are going. The gospel restores dignity to humanity and lifts man from the bondage of sin to the very right hand of God.

It is God's chosen method to release His saving power to every person on the earth. As Paul continued:

For I am not ashamed of the gospel of Christ, for it is the power of God to salvation for everyone who believes....

—Romans 1:16

The gospel is not an inferior message or an outdated method. It is the power of God unto salvation to everyone who believes. There is nothing else like it, and nothing else can do what the gospel can do. It is more powerful than radio-active material. It is the spiritual nuclear option. It goes beyond the flesh and the physical world and reaches the spirit of man, where its power produces true salvation and radical change. When the gospel is accurately presented to a man or woman and he or she believes it, the impact on them is eternal. Gospel truth is the only substance in the world that has this effect on the lives of people.

We are commissioned to share this Good News. Jesus told us to "go into all the world and preach the gospel to every creature" (Mark 16:15). Every creature means every person. No matter where we go or who we meet—whether it's a businessman in the urban jungle or a tribesman in the Amazon jungle—this gospel is for everyone. Wherever we go, it will work on whomever cares to listen.

God is no respecter of persons. What Jesus did, He did for everyone. There will be people from every race and nation who come into the family of God. The book of Revelation reveals this truth in the words of the song of the redeemed that will be sung in heaven:

And they sang a new song, saying: "You are worthy to take the scroll, And to open its seals; For You were slain, And have redeemed us to God by Your blood Out of every tribe and tongue and people and nation, And have made us kings and priests to our God; And we shall reign on the earth."

—Revelation 5:9-10

"We have the opportunity to share the Good News with our generation and continue to gather a harvest of souls, the precious fruit of the earth."

The gospel will work for every tribe and tongue and people and nation, for God so loved the world. Heaven will be filled with all the different people groups who have ever lived on the earth. We have the opportunity to share the Good News with our generation and continue to gather a harvest of souls, the precious fruit of the earth.

What a privilege it is to share this message!

But we have this treasure in earthen vessels, that the excellence of the power may be of God and not of us.

—2 Corinthians 4:7

The gospel is a treasure, and we are the guardians of this treasure. We must be faithful to its message.

> *Let a man so consider us, as servants of Christ and stewards of the mysteries of God. Moreover it is required in stewards that one be found faithful.*
>
> —1 Corinthians 4:1-2

The New Living Translation says of the same verses:

> *…servants of Christ who have been put in charge of explaining God's mysteries. Now, a person who is put in charge as a manager must be faithful*
>
> —1 Corinthians 4:1-2 (NLT)

The answer has come, and it must be offered to everyone. We have been put in charge of spreading this message and sharing God's saving power with the world. We do it with words. The gospel is shared, transmitted, transferred from person to person, nation to nation and generation to generation with words. When these words are spoken, they have within them the power to save the lost and heal the sick. Wherever the gospel is preached and believed, lives are changed. This is an ingenious plan, and it works splendidly.

You don't have to carry God's blessings in a trunk or container, a box car or a cargo ship. You can take His wonderful saving power anywhere in the world with words. God's saving power is contained in the message you already have in your heart.

GOOD NEWS

Be confident in the message. It's our message.

It is the best news in the world. Speak the gospel. Teach the gospel. Preach the gospel, and let it do its awesome work in the lives of people.

Let's plunder the kingdom of darkness and fill heaven with a new generation of converts!

Let's let the world know the Good News is so good the bad news doesn't matter.

A GIFT FOR YOU

If you are looking for a change in your life or if you are seeking a peace that is found through a personal relationship with a loving God, then He is ready and willing to help you—right now, and right where you are.

Salvation is a gift that is made available to those who repent, believe and confess that Jesus is Lord, and He died and rose from the dead to save mankind (Acts 16:31; Romans 10:9-10). This gift cannot be received through good deeds or by simply being a good person (Ephesians 2:8, 1 Timothy 1:9). It's received by faith—by believing and acting on God's Word concerning salvation.

Pray this prayer aloud, now:

> *Heavenly Father, I come to You in the name of Jesus. Your Word says, "…Whoever calls on the name of the Lord shall be saved" (Acts 2:21). I am calling on You.*
>
> *I pray and ask Jesus to come into my heart and be Lord and Savior over my life. According*

to Romans 10:9-10, "...If you confess with your mouth the Lord Jesus and believe in your heart that God has raised Him from the dead, you will be saved."

I do that now. I confess Jesus as my Lord, and I believe in my heart that God raised Him from the dead.

If you have prayed this prayer, welcome to the family of God!

Share your good news with us! Please take a minute to give us your name and address, and let us know what God has done in your life.

 **Greg Fritz Ministries**

For more information about Greg Fritz Ministries or a listing of additional teaching materials, visit www.gregfritz.org or write to us at P.O. Box 700900, Tulsa, OK 74170.

The Harrison House Vision

Proclaiming the truth and the power
of the Gospel of Jesus Christ with excellence.
Challenging Christians
to live victoriously,
grow spiritually,
know God intimately.

Connect with us on

f Facebook @ HarrisonHousePublishers

and **◙** Instagram @ HarrisonHousePublishing

so you can stay up to date with news

about our books and our authors.

Visit us at **www.harrisonhouse.com**

for a complete product listing as well as

monthly specials for wholesale distribution.